Frederick George Lee

Paraphrastica expositio articulorum confessionis Anglicanae

The articles of the Anglican church paraphrastically considered and explained

Frederick George Lee

Paraphrastica expositio articulorum confessionis Anglicanae
The articles of the Anglican church paraphrastically considered and explained

ISBN/EAN: 9783337259761

Printed in Europe, USA, Canada, Australia, Japan

Cover: Foto ©Lupo / pixelio.de

More available books at **www.hansebooks.com**

Paraphrastica Expositio Articulorum Confessionis Anglicanae:

THE ARTICLES OF THE ANGLICAN CHURCH

PARAPHRASTICALLY CONSIDERED AND EXPLAINED,

BY

FRANCISCUS A. SANCTA CLARA, S.T.P.

(DR. CHRISTOPHER DAVENPORT.)

Reprinted from the Edition in Latin of 1646, with a Translation, together with Expositions and Comments in English from the Theological Problems and Propositions of the same writer, and with additional Notes and References.

TO WHICH ARE PREFIXED

AN INTRODUCTION AND A SKETCH OF THE LIFE OF THE AUTHOR.

EDITED BY THE REV.

FREDERICK GEORGE LEE, D.C.L.,

F.S.A. LOND. AND SCOT.; S.C.L. OXON.; DOMESTIC CHAPLAIN TO THE EARL OF MORTON.

London:
JOHN T. HAYES, LYALL PLACE, EATON SQUARE, S.W.

MDCCCLXV.

"Such interpretation may be given of the most difficult Articles as will strip them of all contradiction to the decrees of the Tridentine Synod."—*Cardinal Wiseman.*

"None can be fairer in theological controversy than SANCTA CLARA; his Commentary on the "Articles," from a Roman Catholic point of view, being especially interesting. It is believed that this remarkable Treatise formed the basis of Mr. NEWMAN's Tract No. 90."—*British Magazine.*

Printed at the Regent Press, 55, King Street, Regent Street, W.

CONTENTS.

	PAGE
Dedication	v
Introduction	vii
Sketch of the Author's Life	xix
Original Dedication	xxxi
Censuræ et Judicia Doctorum	xxxiii

THE ARTICLES PARAPHRASTICALLY EXPLAINED:—

Article I.—Of Faith in the Holy Trinity	1
II.—Of the Word or Son of God, Which was made very Man	1
III.—Of the going down of Christ into Hell	2
IV.—Of the Resurrection of Christ	2
V.—Of the Holy Ghost	2
VI.—Of the Sufficiency of the Holy Scriptures for Salvation	3
VII.—Of the Old Testament	7
VIII.—Of the Three Creeds	8
IX.—Of Original or Birth-sin	8
X.—Of Free-Will	10
XI.—Of the Justification of Man	11
XII.—Of Good Works	14
XIII.—Of Works before Justification	14
XIV.—Of Works of Supererogation	16
XV.—Of Christ alone without Sin	17
XVI.—Of Sin after Baptism	21

	PAGE
Article XVII.—Of Predestination and Election	24
XVIII.—Of obtaining Eternal Salvation only by the Name of Christ	26
XIX.—Of the Church	27
XX.—Of the Authority of the Church	29
XXI.—Of the Authority of General Councils	32
XXII.—Of Purgatory	39
XXIII.—Of Ministering in the Congregation	42
XXIV.—Of speaking in the Congregation in such a tongue as the people understandeth	42
XXV.—Of the Sacraments	49
XXVI.—Of the Unworthiness of the Ministers, which hinders not the effect of the Sacrament	53
XXVII.—Of Baptism	54
XXVIII.—Of the Lord's Supper	55
XXIX.—Of the wicked which eat not the Body of Christ in the use of the Lord's Supper	63
XXX.—Of both kinds	68
XXXI.—Of the one Oblation of Christ finished upon the Cross	73
XXXII.—Of the Marriage of Priests	79
XXXIII.—Of Excommunicate persons, how they are to be avoided	80
XXXIV.—Of the Traditions of the Church	81
XXXV.—Of the Homilies	83
XXXVI.—Of Consecration of Bishops and Ministers	85
XXXVII.—Of the Civil Magistrates	96
XXXVIII.—Of Christian Men's Goods, which are not common	115
XXXIX.—Of a Christian Man's Oath	115

TO

AMBROSE LISLE MARCHE PHILLIPPS DE LISLE, ESQUIRE,

OF GARENDON PARK AND GRACE DIEU MANOR, LEICESTERSHIRE,

ETC., ETC.

MY DEAR MR. DE LISLE,

I know no one to whom I can more fittingly inscribe this reprint of Sancta Clara's Treatise than yourself. For more than thirty years past you have laboured for the high and holy object of Re-union; while the rise and expansion in England of what is now something more than a "school," systematically praying and working for this object, is a testimony as well to your charity and farsightedness as to the fact that a common desire for Peace and Unity is the first step towards obtaining them. Therefore, with very sincere respect and regard—*in spem Unionis Futuræ Gregis Christi*—I dedicate this volume to you.

And I remain,

Ever most sincerely yours in our Blessed LORD,

FREDERICK GEORGE LEE.

INTRODUCTION.

THE true position of the Thirty-Nine Articles in the Church of England is one worthy of especial remark. They are clearly not "Articles *of Faith*,"*—that is, they are not a portion of the unalterable divine deposit delivered at Pentecost, which a man rejects at the peril of salvation,—but "Articles *of Religion*," as they are generally termed,—that is, they may be regarded as a collection of propositions concerning Religion and Religious opinions† drawn up in the sixteenth century, a few of which contain articles of faith, some matters of fact or historical assertions, and others certain opinions upon which the post-Reformation clergy have always differed very considerably.‡ This will be clear from the following :—"When it is said that S. Jerome expresses a particular opinion respecting the Apocrypha; that a certain Greek term has been expounded in four different manners; that certain churches have erred; that the Pelagians hold a particular doctrine; that S. Augustine holds a particular view respecting the participation of the Holy Eucharist by the

---

* Vide Pearson *On the Creed*, p. 17, *et seq.* Oxford: 1847.

† "They are to the Creeds what the bye-laws of a society are to the legal and settled rules of that society."—Dr. W. H. Mill.

‡ Compare, *e. g.* Bps. Burnet, Beveridge, and Harold Browne on those Articles which have been explained fully by Sancta Clara. Their differences of explanation are great and singular.

wicked; that the Injunctions of Elizabeth do most plainly testify to a certain fact; that school authors say that the works of the unregenerate deserve grace of congruity;—these are all historical assertions, which may or may not be true, but which we cannot be called upon to hold with a divine faith. Thus, when the Book of Homilies ascribes a real existence to Pope Joan, it makes an historical assertion which is now known to be false. So, again, when we are told that it is impossible for Christ's natural body to be at the same time in more places than one,—this is merely a philosophical opinion, which may or may not be true, and which we are neither concerned to defend nor to attack."*

Not one of these statements, be it remarked, is a matter of faith; nor is it of faith to receive a particular explanation of a text of Scripture. Nor again, when the eighth Article maintains that the Three Catholic Creeds are to be believed *because* "they may be proved by most certain warrants of Holy Scripture," are we called upon to accept the Creeds on this ground. Still less, when in the twenty-sixth Article it is maintained, "They that receive them [the Sacraments] unworthily, purchase to themselves damnation, as St. Paul saith," are we at all bound to hold that the apostle was referring to Baptism also in the passage to which this Article alludes.

Again: (I.) To discover how numerous are the propositions, both positive and negative, contained in the Articles which, *ex necessitate rei*, cannot possibly be of faith; or (II.), still further, how almost impossible it is for Anglican clergy of the present

---

* Neale's *Lectures on Church Difficulties*, p. 190. London: Cleaver, 1852.

day to estimate accurately the value of other propositions, the following obvious examples may be instanced:—

I. 1. "The Riches and Goods of Christians are not common." (Not a matter of faith.)
 2. "General Councils may not be gathered together without the commandment and will of princes." (Not a matter of faith.)
 3. "The Bishop of Rome hath * no jurisdiction in this realm of England." (Neither a fact, nor a matter of faith.)
 4. "Transubstantiation is repugnant to the plain words of Scripture." (Not a matter of faith.)

II. "The second Book of Homilies† . . . . doth contain a godly and wholesome doctrine and necessary for these times." (This is certainly not a matter of faith. As to its accuracy as a mere statement with reference to the needs of the sixteenth century, we are not called upon to enter upon an examination of its truth or in any way to express an opinion on the subject. The book may or may not contain "Godly and wholesome doctrine," and the "Godly and whole-

---

* Even before the passing of the Roman Catholic Emancipation Bill, Vicars Apostolic exercised jurisdiction on behalf of the Pope in England, and received obedience. Since that change, both in England and Ireland the lawful spiritual authority of Roman bishops has been and is allowed, and indirectly sanctioned by law.

† "If we are to be tied to the Homilies as to a Confession of Faith, we must believe in the divine right of kings, in the inspiration of the Apocrypha, in the benefit of a fish diet, in the anti-Christianity of the Pope, and in the binding authority of the example of the early Church. Does any one man believe in all these things together?"—Neale's *Lectures on Church Difficulties*, p. 200.

some doctrine" may or may not have been necessary for the times when the Articles were drawn up.)

Though the Articles are generally supposed to run counter to the doctrines and principles of Latin Christianity, yet it is remarkable how ingeniously—perhaps it would be more accurate to say how vaguely they are worded. This policy was no doubt adopted to retain all schools in the National Church, as Bishop Burnet, the Erastian, and Dr. Beveridge both allow. So, notwithstanding the existence of expressions which *appear* strong at first sight and before they are carefully examined, there can be little doubt, as both Sancta Clara and *Tract* 90 proved, that there are few propositions which may not be brought into perfect harmony with the current opinions of the rest of Western Christendom. There is nothing against the doctrine of the Sacrifice of the Mass, or, as we commonly term it, the Sacrifice of the Holy Eucharist,—there is not a word (if we omit the obvious truisms set forth in the last paragraph of Article 25) against Reservation, nor a sentiment derogatory of Confession. Very frequently we hear statements that the Church of England condemns " the idolatry of Rome." Yet is there a single syllable on this point in the Thirty-Nine Articles from end to end? The strongest statement in any way bearing on the subject is that the "Romish doctrine" concerning the worshipping of images *inter alia* "is a fond thing vainly invented" (*res est futilis*—useless —*inaniter conficta*), but this is all.

It was calculated by a painstaking writer of the seventeenth century, Mr. R. Shelton, one of the foremost in the Laudian Revival, that the Articles contained about 670 distinct proposi-

tions, of which about 150 only were of a positive character, the remainder being simply negations.* The Dean of St. Paul's recently repeated this remark, with the object of suggesting the relaxation or abolition of subscription—a work of great importance to every school of thought in the Church of England, more especially to those who desire to promote the Visible Re-union of Christendom. "If I venture," writes Dean Milman, "to question the expediency, the wisdom, I will say the righteousness (that word contains in itself and overrides both the former) of retaining subscription to the Thirty-Nine Articles as obligatory on all clergymen, I do so, not from any difficulty in reconciling with my own conscience what, during my life, I have done more than once, but from the deep and deliberate conviction that such subscription is altogether unnecessary as a safeguard for the essential doctrines of Christianity, which are more safely and fully protected by other means. It never has been, is not, and never will be a solid security for its professed object, the reconciling or removing religious differences, which it tends rather to create and keep alive; is embarrassing to many men who might be of the most valuable service in the ministry of the Church; is objectionable as concentrating and enforcing the attention of the youngest clergy on questions, some

---

* "The story of Charles V. and the clocks is well known. A recent illustration of the same difficulty occurred not long ago, when a celebrated theologian expressed his 'utter amazement' that 80 men of various sentiments could have been able to subscribe their assent to three or four brief propositions contained in a memorial on an academical examination What would he have said had he for the first time heard of not 80, but 20,000 persons subscribing their assent to at least 600 propositions on the most intricate and complex subjects that can engage the human mind?"—*Stanley on Subscription*, p. 15.

abstruse, some antiquated (more of this hereafter), and in themselves at once so minute and so comprehensive as to harass less instructed and profound thinkers, to perplex and tax the sagacity of the most able lawyers and the most learned divines."—*Fraser's Magazine*, p. 269, March, 1865. Furthermore, it should be remembered that the Articles do not stand in the same relation to the Anglican Church as do the Decrees of the Council of Trent to Roman Catholics, or the Acts of the Synod of Bethlehem to members of the orthodox Eastern Church. Roman Catholics hold the Council of Trent to have been an Œcumenical Council, because—from their point of view—(1) the whole Church was represented at it, and (2) it was amongst them universally received. Consequently they regard the creed of Pope Pius as of equal weight with the other creeds. And the same is practically the case with the Decrees of the Synod of Bethlehem, generally accepted in the East—a Synod at which the various anthropological* propositions set forth at Trent were in the main and substantially received by the Oriental communion. But, on our part, no one ever dreamt of regarding the Synods of London in 1559 and 1571 as anything more than mere national synods—as, therefore, claiming no power to define, declare, or propound Articles of Faith, and consequently incompetent to add a series of theological opinions—both negative and positive—to the original deposit,—to the three ancient and universally-received creeds. This being so, and experience having taught those who have looked for a Future Visible Re-union of the Christian Family that

---

* Vide Ffoulkes' *Christendom's Divisions*, in loco. London: Longmans, 1865; and Oxenham *on the Atonement*, p. xliv. London: Longmans, 1865.

the multiplication of religious tests and propositions is the source of untold mischief, the recent manifestos in the Church of England favourable to the quiet removal of the Thirty-Nine Articles deserve the careful attention and proper respect of all theological schools. If to-morrow they were abolished utterly and absolutely—with their multifarious propositions and apparent contradictions—the faith of the Church of England would remain just as it is. No single iota of the Truth of God would be lost. "I believe in . . . the Holy Catholic Church." "I believe One [Holy] Catholic and Apostolic Church." "Whosoever will be saved, before all things it is necessary that he hold the Catholic Faith," would still be the utterance of the faithful in our ancient sanctuaries, and we should have removed the single great difficulty, on our part, in the way of effecting that intercommunion for which so many constantly hope and pray.

Mr. Ffoulkes, in his recent valuable and masterly work, *Christendom's Divisions*, has entered at some length upon a consideration of certain of the Thirty-Nine Articles. His opinion of them is all the more important as he himself formerly belonged to the Church of England. Moreover, the singular fairness and impartiality displayed throughout his remarks, and the obvious desire never to overstate his case, give great and unusual weight to the following interesting comments:—

"From which remark I pass straight to the Thirty-nine Articles, because they do not stop there but go some steps further in advance. The Prayer Book condemns rather by implication and by its silence. The Articles attack openly, and with no small virulence, doctrines and practices which, till then, had been current in the English Church and in the West generally. They may not have been framed in overt hostility to the Decrees of Trent,

whose actual promulgation they just anticipated. They may not have been copied from the Confession of Augsburg, which came out so much earlier, or by the Synod of Dort, which followed so much later; but they established a breach with the past equally grave **and** premeditated, and which in all **English** constitutional history, from Egbert to Queen Victoria, **can** have but one name—Treason!

"Previously to their publication, or rather previously to that rupture with Rome which led to it, the Church of England had for upwards of 1200 years—almost twice **as long as England** had then been a monarchy—been associated by federal ties of the closest nature with that world-wide corporation known as the Catholic Church, and had participated to the fullest extent in all its vicissitudes and successive developments. As far back as A.D. 347, bishops from Britain are mentioned as having been present at the Council of Sardica, where **they must have been parties** to those canons authorising **appeals in certain cases to the see of Rome**; and where, **from the** very nature **of the** case, they could not fail to have heard that earlier canon talked about, of which the historian of the **Greek** Church, Socrates, speaks, declaring it unlawful for any local churches to make canons against the will of the bishop of that see. Twelve years from that date they were congratulated by S. Hilary on having preserved their orthodoxy; two years more, and they were noticed at the Council of Rimini. The century following, aided by two bishops from France, they made common cause with the rest of the Church against Pelagianism.* Before the end of the next century, S. Augustine had founded the **see** of Canterbury, which in process of time came to be acknowledged as the metropolitan church of the whole island, and even of Ireland, as we have seen. The bishops of Scotland for a time went to York, and the bishops of Ireland to Canterbury, for consecration. The archbishops of Canterbury, without one exception, for nine centuries **and** upwards, among **the sixty-three who held that see** down to Cranmer inclusive, received their palls from Rome.

"When East and West separated, it was the Primate of all England who, by command of the **Pope**, undertook the cause of the whole West, before a **synod** held in its extreme frontier-town on the Italian coast—Bari. When

---

* "Collier, E. H., vol. i. pp. 69-112. His remarks on the Sardican Canons are special pleading."

East and West were thought to have been happily reunited once more, tidings were sent to, and congratulatory letters were received from, and public rejoicings throughout his dominions were decreed by, the youthful King of England, Henry VI.: copies of which exist still in the archiepiscopal archives,* in token that the heart of England beat in active sympathy with the rest of Christendom. It was not merely that the see of Canterbury was mindful of its primeval obligations, or its canonical duties to the see of Rome. No General Council was ever summoned from which the bishops of England were left out: no General Council ever promulgated any decrees, which from the time of their acceptance in England were not made part-and-parcel of the ecclesiastical law of that realm. Now and then there were delays in recognising a pope, or in accepting the decrees of a council—as, for instance, of Basle. Now and then there were the usual disputes in connection with both, incidental to the parts of every corporate body.

"Such had been the prescriptive rights and obligations of the Church of England for upwards of 1200 years, when the Prayer Book was compiled, and the Thirty-nine Articles promulgated as its future doctrinal tests. There had been a quarrel between one king of England, Henry VIII., and one pope, Clement VII., of a personal character, affecting at most the domestic happiness of the former; just as there must always be when individuals involve themselves in any civil or ecclesiastical suit, and it had proceeded to extremities on both sides. But never had the Pope threatened any encroachments, then, on the abstract rights of the Crown; still less had there been any attack on the liberties of the Church of England. There had been no new doctrine promulgated, nor any new discipline enjoined for acceptance by it. Because a monarch, so notoriously singular as Henry VIII. in his matrimonial arrangements, had been thwarted in them, the Church of England assented to abjure the supremacy of the Pope in that reign, to burn and destroy all its time-honoured rituals for celebrating Divine service in the next; and then, after a few years of feigned repentance under Mary, reproduced, under Elizabeth, its new 'Service Book' and

---

* "Lambeth, 211, Nos. 98, 99. The first is dated 'Our Camp at Windsor,' A.D. 1439, Oct. 3, and is on the reunion of the Greeks; the second is earlier, 'From Reading Convent,' Feb. 8, A.D. 1439, and is on the reunion of the Armenians with the Western Church."

Articles of 'Religion:' not only without the smallest reference to the opinions of the rest of Christendom, but in open defiance of the General Council of the West, then actually sitting, and to which its bishops among others had, in conformity with ancient usage, received their summons—all which it justified on the ground that it had resolved, for the future, to be quit of the Pope.

"Now, even at this point it might have halted, without any further outrage upon the constitutional prerogatives of every corporate society. It scorned the idea of any such moderation. Transubstantiation, which for more than three centuries it had held and taught, in conformity with the Fourth Lateran Council, it now condemned as 'repugnant to the plain words of Scripture.' Purgatory, which it had maintained with the Council of Florence against the Greek doctrine on that subject, it now discarded as 'a vain invention.' Restriction of the cup to the celebrant priest, which it had received from the Council of Constance, it now asserted to be contrary to 'Christ's ordinance.' Celibacy of the clergy, which in common with the rest of the West had been its own discipline from time immemorial, it now declared it to be lawful to depart from, though no other Western Church had relaxed that rule. To teach that there were seven sacraments, as all previous archbishops of York and Canterbury must have done more or less, it now regarded as a product of 'the corrupt following of the Apostles.' To ask for the prayers of the Saints in heaven, to venerate their relics and images on earth, as the Church of Rome did, it affirmed to be 'repugnant to the Word of God;' though its old office-books alone showed how identical had been its own authorised practice, from the Norman Conquest at latest. Finally, in consenting to abandon appeals to Rome, it repudiated not merely one of the first principles of its own Canon Law, but likewise one of the earliest synodical acts on record of its own primitive bishops, above 1200 years previously, who sat and voted at that council which authorised them. All this it did without so much as asking counsel or inviting criticism from any one of the local churches in Europe—with all which it had for so long been united as one family—on the wisdom or justice of its proceedings. The only foreigners whom it condescended to consult at all were those who had unchurched themselves. In that one respect, that of taking a bold line of its own, it may have acted as England usually does : in all other respects how thoroughly un-English was the course pursued ! The questions which

it reopened and the points which it retracted had no reference to the decrees of any one council that had been held, or to any one dogma that had been put forward, of late years. France was slow to accept the Council of Trent from the first, and has never accepted it wholly to this day. All the Trullan Canons, and even the three last canons of the Council of Chalcedon, were rejected by the Holy See, and have never since been received. The Greeks demurred to the addition of the word 'Filioque' to the creed at once, and have never really given in. But here was a local church arrogating to set aside doctrines and practices of the collective Church—which it had for ages accepted, inculcated, and enforced itself—on the ground principally that they were 'repugnant to the Word of God;' but only, therefore, as interpreted by its own living authorities of that one period. What must have been the unavoidable inference suggested to the minds of all intelligent thinkers? If for five, if for ten centuries all the bishops and theologians of the collective Church were proved to have known nothing of the true meaning of the Word of God, how many degrees below nothing might the living authorities of one local church of a single age be supposed to rank in their estimate of the same? Had each of the English counties taken that view of their constitutional obligations in the sixteenth century, what would have been the condition of Old England now? Had each of the Churches of Europe followed the example of the Church of England, what would have become of the unity of the Catholic Church by this time?"—(Chap. 87, pp. 216-220.)

We here learn the deliberate opinions of a Roman Catholic thoroughly competent to form a true judgment with reference to the Articles—opinions which are no doubt shared by many, and deserve the careful consideration of members of the Church of England. They are most valuable as indicating with exactness the particular reform which is most pressingly required in the first instance, and point out what kind of work must be undertaken in a spirit of boldness and charity to effect that Visible Re-union amongst the separated portions of the Christian Family so earnestly desired. May it please God that all needless

bars and hindrances to this blessed consummation be speedily and completely removed!

Since the publication of *Tract* 90—which was currently reported to have been more or less founded upon Sancta Clara's work—some desire has existed amongst members of the Church of England to be possessed of this remarkable treatise. It is now re-published, therefore, as it was originally written, in Latin, together with an English translation, in parallel columns. It has been printed from the London edition * (fcp. 8vo), without publisher's name, of 1646, the text of which has been carefully compared with that of the Lyons edition (small 4to), issued by Anthony Chard,—both extremely rare. For the gift of the first the editor is indebted to a friend; for the loan of the second to the Rev. J. P. Kane, M.A. The extracts from the explanatory Problems are given in English only: they will be found at length (and most valuable reading they are) in all the editions of Sancta Clara's book, *Deus, Natura, Gratia, etc.* The editor is especially grateful for, and desires to acknowledge with sincere thanks, the great help afforded him by the Rev. Henry de Romestin, M.A., of St. John's College, Oxford, now of Freiburg in Breisgau, in the preparation of this reprint; and also expresses his obligation for assistance rendered by his friends the Rev. Dr. Littledale and the Rev. H. N. Oxenham, M.A., in looking over the proof sheets.

* This edition is neither in the Bodleian nor British Museum.

19, COLESHILL STREET, EATON SQUARE, S.W.
St. Bernard's Day, August 20th, 1865.

SKETCH OF THE AUTHOR'S LIFE.

THE AUTHOR of this interesting and remarkable treatise, Christopher Davenport, whose name in religion was Franciscus à Sancta Clara—known also as Francis Hunt, Francis Coventrie, or Francis of Coventry—is said, by Antony à Wood,[*] to have been the fifth son of Henry Davenport, alderman of Coventry, the grandson to a younger brother of the Davenports of Cheshire.[†] He was born at Coventry about the year 1598, and "in grammar learning there educated." When about fifteen years of age, in company with a brother, John, he was matriculated at Merton College, Oxford, in the early part of the year 1613—both being pupils of Mr. Samuel Lane, fellow of that society. Sir Henry Savile, then Warden of Merton, is said to have dismissed both the Davenports, because they were poor and unable formally to become commoners of the college—the result being that John Davenport went to Magdalen Hall, and afterwards became a noted Puritan; while Christopher, after remaining some time longer (during Sir Henry's sojourn at Eton), a pupil of Mr. Lane, of Merton College, was induced by some Roman Catholic

---

[*] *Athenæ Oxoniensis*, ed. Bliss, vol. iii. p. 1221. London 1817.

[†] The Davenports of Davenport, Woodford, and Bramhall, co. Chester, were a very ancient family. They bore for their arms, argent, a chevron sable between three cross-crosslets fitché of the second. Crest, on a wreath a felon's head couped proper, haltered or. In the Visitation of the County Palatine of Chester the name of Christopher Davenport occurs more than once: *e.g.*, Christopher Davenport, seventh son of John Davenport, of Woodford, Esq., and Mary [daughter of Hugh Bromley, of Hampton Post, Esq.] was baptized at Prestbury, co. Lancaster, 20th Sept. 1612.

clergyman, who is believed to have resided in or near Oxford, to join the Roman Church and go to Douay. Having taken this step he remained there for some time, but afterwards went to Ypres, where he was received into the order of the Franciscans on the 7th of October, 1617. Returning to Douay, he was—as Antony à Wood declares—"entered into the English Recollects* there of the same order," on the 18th October, 1618. Continuing his course of study in the College of St. Bonaventure, he afterwards went into Spain. At the ancient University of Salamanca he improved himself very much in the supreme faculty, returning some time later to Douay, where he studied philosophy, and eventually became chief reader in theology, guardian of the convent, and was created Professor of Sacred Theology (S.T.P.). Some time after this, at the request of certain members of the Franciscan

---

* My learned friend, the Provost of Northampton, has kindly given me the following interesting account of the English Franciscan Recollects at Douay, which I gladly print as it reached me:—"This establishment originated with the Rev. John Gennings, a Douay priest, in the year 1614. He was desirous to revive the Franciscan Order among the English; and with that view received the habit from William Stanney, sub-Commissary-General of the Franciscan province in England. He induced several students at Douay and the other English colleges to follow his example; and these went through their noviceship at Ypres. F. Gennings, in 1616, in quality of vicar and custos of England, assembled about half a dozen brethren, including novices, at Gravelines, and within three years they succeeded in establishing at Douay the Convent of St. Bonaventure, with a noviceship attached. Few in number, destitute of endowment, and depending solely on alms, they still contrived to erect a handsome church. In 1624 the number of members resident was fifteen. In the following year F. Francis, of St. Clare (Davenport) was sent to Rome to obtain the restoration of the English province. He was partially successful; and four years later the restoration was completed, and they were declared by the Minister General of the Order, F. Bernardine de Senis, sufficiently numerous to be entitled to the privileges of a separate province, of which F. Gennings was appointed provincial; and this restoration was sanctioned and confirmed by the authority of the Holy See. F. Gennings died at Douay, November 2nd, 1660, of his religious profession 46. Their object was to prepare labourers for the English Mission; they enjoyed the privileges of the university of Douay. In 1700 they had 60 members, and continued to flourish till the French Revolution in 1793; but all the friars found means to escape out of France in disguise.—F. C. H."

order in England,* he was induced to leave his work in France and to undertake missionary labours in his native country, where he was generally known by his name in religion of Franciscus à Sancta Clara, and rendered very efficient services by his literary works to the cause to which he had devoted himself. He was appointed one of the Chaplains to Her Majesty Queen Henrietta Maria, the royal consort of King Charles the First, and soon became as highly and deservedly honoured for his learning, ability, and devotion by members of the Church of England as he was by the leading authorities of his own communion. During the considerable period of fifty years he was constantly and in many ways devoted to the important work of re-Catholicising those in whom the errors of Wycliffe, Luther and Calvin, together with the unbridled licence of more recent troublous times, had gone far to destroy their faith. He raised money to carry on the work of Christian education at Douay and elsewhere, while the last list of his works testifies both to his unwearied labours and considerable theological knowledge. During the whole period of the Great Rebellion, when both Roman Catholics and members of the Church of England suffered so severely, he laboured continually, from his own point of view, to preserve the ancient faith among those families which had never cast it off; and strove, at the same time, to gain the active support of the most distinguished prelates and theologians of the National Church, for co-operation in promoting a visible corporate Re-union. He was in constant communication with Archbishop Laud,† Bishop Montague, Dr. Cosin, and others of that influential school; and, on one occasion, made application through Dr. Augustus Lindsell, one of the Archbishop's chaplains, to have a book in defence of Episcopacy—*Apologia Episcoporum seu Sacri Magistratus propugnatio, etc.*—formally licensed for printing. Sancta Clara was found sometimes in London,

---

* The Minister-General of the Franciscans, by Letters Patent, dated from Madrid 6th of August, 1629, announced the formal restoration of the English province.

† Laud's *History of His Troubles*, p. 430. Ed. 1695. London.

but more frequently in Oxford, where he was always received most kindly by Mr. Thomas Barloe, chief librarian of the Bodleian—all the services of whom are fully acknowledged in a general way in more than one of his publications. To members of the Church of England his most interesting work is that which is here reprinted—an attempt (and a very successful attempt) to reconcile various propositions in the Thirty-nine Articles with the general belief of the rest of Western Christendom. He obviously desired, and laboured for, a corporate Re-union; and practically took one of the most important and efficient steps towards effecting it, that could possibly have been chosen, by showing men on both sides, even at that period, that they already agreed more, and differed less, than the prejudice of popular opinion would have them believe; and, furthermore, that many of those points on which they differed were rather of the accidents than the substance of Divine Truth. His Treatise, which was dedicated to King Charles the First, on its appearance created a great sensation. The Puritans, who ran in the narrowest of narrow grooves, disliked and maligned the great principle of divine charity on which it was founded. The school of Laud and Cosin, of Shelford and Pocklington, appeared unprepared to accept its line of argument and conclusions, if a true judgment can be formed from the various attitudes taken up by different writers who put themselves forward to reply to it. Amongst his own co-religionists, many were found who questioned the wisdom of his policy, because they were unprepared to allow the Church of England all that he had assumed it still retained and possessed. Others, again, saw in his Christian temper and moderation much to commend; and for the future were of good courage and hopeful. For the general tone and feeling of the clergy were rapidly changing, as Davenport had long ago discovered at Oxford; while the dreary Calvinism and mischievous Erastianism under Elizabeth had given place to principles far more nearly approaching those of the ancient system than had ever energized since the evil days of separation and division under Henry the Eighth. Father Leander, a friend and contemporary of Sancta Clara, who had been specially sent to enquire into the true state of the Church of

England, fully testifies to this change, and especially to her character as entirely distinct from that of foreign Protestant sects.* It is no wonder, therefore, that when a small section of Roman Catholics in England attempted to obtain a formal condemnation of Sancta Clara's book, the King, who had been its patron, whose sympathies were entirely in a Catholic direction, and who longed for Re-union,†—gave a special commission to the Queen's agent at Rome to prevent so unfortunate a mistake being committed.‡ Through the over-zealous partizanship of certain persons who appeared unable to comprehend rightly the great object which its author entertained, and so charitably desired to see accomplished, several attempts to bring it under the censure of the "Holy Office" were made, but failed. Amongst Clarendon's *State Papers* § a Letter from Rome from "John Selbye" to Father Leander—who styles himself elsewhere "F. Leander de S. Martino, Congregationis Angliæ Benedictinorum

---

* "They [*i.e.*, members of the Church of England] agree in all the doctrine of the Trinity, and Incarnation and True Deity of our Blessed Saviour; in the points of Providence, predestination, justification, necessity of good works, co-operation of freewill with the grace of God: they admit the first four General Councils, the three authentic symbols, of the Apostles, Nice or Constantinople, and of St. Athanasius, as they are received in the Roman Church; they reverence the Primitive Church, and unanimous consent of the ancient fathers, and all traditions and ceremonies which can be sufficiently proved by testimony of antiquity; they admit a settled Liturgy, taken out of the Roman Liturgy, distinction of orders, bishops, priests, and deacons, in distinct habits from the laity, and divers other points in which no transmarine Protestants do agree."—Father Leander's *Report of the State and Character of the Church of England* (A.D. 1634), addressed to Cardinal Barberino. — Clarendon's *State Papers*, vol. i., p. 207.

† From the "Instructions" given by His Majesty King Charles to Captain Arthur Brett, sent to Rome as agent of the Queen (A.D. 1635): "You may of yourself, as you will find occasion, insinuate that as the Pope is a Temporal Prince, we shall not be unwilling to join with him, as we do with other Catholic Roman Princes, in anything that may conduce to the peace of Christendom and to the visible Re-union of the Church."

‡ Letter from —— to —— (vol. i. p. 171, Clarendon's *State Papers*):—"You desired me to do what possibly I could to stop their proceedings at Rome against Mr. W How and Mr. Francis de Sancta Clara's Books, lest the State should be exasperated in case the Cardinals should pass any censure against them upon your word. I did so."

§ Clarendon's *State Papers*, vol. i., p. 168.

Præses generalis,"—contains the following :—" The event of Father Francis Clare's Book will be that it will be forbidden : yet in the modestest kind, to give His Majesty satisfaction, who is exceedingly beloved and esteemed here, by great and little, for his virtues, of which all sorts give abundant commendations ; and for this same reason they will not proceed against the author's person, as they intended. This *was* their intention, but the prolonging of their prohibiting causes some suspicion of alteration in their designs. For me I have always urged that respect be had to His Majesty, and that the book should not be forbid, and this I protest sincerely unto you, upon my salvation." According to Mr. John Selbye, therefore, it was neither the merits nor demerits of the book which were under discussion, but altogether another consideration. In a letter from Rome, which was addressed to Mr. Secretary Windebank, and is endorsed by him, dated Nov. 15, 1634, the writer tells us who John Selbye was :—" Our Procurator in Rome is called by his proper name, Richard Reade, and is a northern man, as I take it, of the Bishoprick of Durham ; but, according to our custom in the Order of S. Bennet, changed his name to Brother Wilfred ; and because the Italians can hardly pronounce that name, he took the name of John Wilfred Selbye, they, upon that, calling him still Fra. Juan Selbye." The case of Sancta Clara, at Rome, is the subject of comment in another letter from Mr. Wilfred (Qy.? Mr. Wilfred, *i.e.*, John Wilfred Selbye) to Father Leander, at p. 250 of the *State Papers;* and again, in a second communication from the same to the same, dated " Rome, May 9, 1635." Some, at least, of his brethren of the Franciscan Order, appear to have disliked Sancta Clara's Treatise, for, in another letter, at p. 336 of the *State Papers*, a detailed account of what was being practically attempted in Italy is set forth :—" Here (at Rome) is arrived one Morton, an English Franciscan, and is already gone to Naples to find the General. I hear, at his return, that he will urge that F. Francis Clara's book be condemned. If I meet him before he makes this proposition, I will strive to divert him from it ; for I see no reason that if His Majesty desires, it should not be forbid but he should have satisfaction." Thus, we mark how

important and valuable was the indirect approbation passed on the book—and on the great principle it embodied. About the same period it received direct and formal approbation from so many independent quarters that it may be almost said to represent the mind of the Roman Catholic communion at the period at which its merits were openly canvassed and determined.

However, in the Rev. Joseph Berington's *Memoirs of Gregorio Panzani* (London: 1813), a work of the greatest interest to all who see the importance of endeavouring to promote the visible Re-union of Christians, this work of Sancta Clara is referred to at length in a passage which gives a somewhat different judgment of its merits, and of the proceedings concerning it, than was delivered by others equally competent to form one. If these *Memoirs* were not actually written by Panzani, he at all events, as Mr. Berington maintains, furnished the materials; it may, therefore, be concluded that the opinion thus placed on record was entertained by some in authority:—" I must here notice a contest which happened concerning the book entitled *Deus, Natura, Gratia*, the author whereof was Mr. Davenport, a Franciscan friar, otherwise called Franciscus à Sancta Clara. This book was highly esteemed by His Majesty, as being full of complaisance for the Protestant* systems in several points, and discovering an inclination of approaching nearer to them by concessions, where the Catholic cause would permit it to be done. But the work was far from being liked at the Roman Court, where it was considered as a very dangerous production, far too condescending to schismatics and heretics. The generality also of the English Catholics were displeased with it. At Rome they proceeded to censure it, though the decree was not made public, the author himself being first summoned to make his appearance, which he declined on account of infirmity, promising to give satisfaction any other way.

---

* Protestant, *i.e.* Church of England. This term had a different meaning in the seventeenth century from that which it bears now. Abp. Laud said he died in the "Protestant faith," meaning of course the faith as taught in the Church of England. Bishops Cosin and Ken used the term in a similar sense.

"This, indeed, was but a private concern, yet it had a public influence, as things then stood. It was the opinion of many that the king was inclined to hearken to terms of an Union between the Two Churches; and that he looked on this book of Davenport as a remote disposition towards it. It was, therefore, deemed an impolitic step in Rome to let their censures loose against it at this juncture. Father Philip was very industrious in acquainting the Roman Court with the inconveniences of rigorous proceedings. He advised them to go on slowly; to wink at the author for a time, alleging that he had submitted himself, and that it would be soon enough to take notice of him when he persisted, or affairs would permit a censure. Soon after, care was taken to inform Windebank that the condemnation was suppressed. But it happening that the author, or some one for him, set forth another edition, in which no submission was expressed, Panzani told the secretary he was afraid the Court of Rome would proceed to a censure, and declare the author contumacious, that the faithful might not be scandalised. The account gave Windebank great concern; and being acquainted with the author, he conferred with him on the subject. They agreed in opinion that the censure would irritate the king, and divert him from any thoughts of an Union. However, to soften the matter, it was given out, and confidently reported, that Mr. Davenport was still prepared to submit himself, and that he had no hand in the second edition, it being the bookseller's contrivance solely for the sake of gain. Windebank also pressed Panzani to take care that they were very cautious at Rome, for that it would certainly ruin all their projects, if a work of that pacific tendency were condemned. But notwithstanding all the care which the author and his friends could take to stifle the censure (which as yet was only privately whispered at Rome), the Jesuits were very busy in publishing it among their acquaintance in England. Davenport then published an *Apology*, wherein he amply declares himself as to the work itself, and submits himself both in that, and all other matters, to the Roman see. He was not, however, willing to leave England; but rather strove to shelter himself under the king's protection, which to some persons appeared to be a very odd

proceeding, and looked as if he designed to go on further. Even some suspected the worst of him, from his having once been a member of the English Church. In the meanwhile Panzani omitted not to advise his Court to be cautious, and to compliment the king in favour of Mr. Davenport, as far as the case would admit."—Pp. 165-168.

At the Restoration of King Charles the Second, when a marriage was celebrated between His Majesty and Catharine of Braganza, Sancta Clara was appointed theologian and one of the Queen's chief chaplains. Five years previously he had been elected, for the third time, Provincial of the English Franciscans,* and at the expiration of his term of office of three years, was again appointed to the same honourable position. Antony à Wood writes that he was "accounted the greatest and chiefest pillar of his order," remarking elsewhere "that he was excellently well versed in school divinity, the Fathers and Councils, philosophers, and in ecclesiastical and profane histories." He is said to have been likewise a person of very pleasing manners, "of free discourse," "of a vivacious and quick countenance," quick of apprehension, and of great accomplishments. His company was greatly sought after by Roman Catholics, and he was held in considerable estimation by members of the Church of England, ever displaying a kindly feeling for those from whom he was separated, and evincing much anxiety to restore to the whole nation that unity of feeling, action, and faith which it had once possessed, having "scarce been broke for a centurie."

As any sketch of the Author's life would be obviously imperfect without a list of his many works, upon which his reputation is founded, and such accounts of them as would enable the reader to discover them for himself, a list is given below, with as much reliable information regarding the particular treatise which is here presented in completeness, as could be obtained :—

---

* "This truly great man succeeded F. Gennings, at the third chapter of the order, in London, 19th June, 1637; was re-appointed by the seventh chapter at Newport, 10th July, 1650; and such was the opinion entertained by his brethren of his experience and merits, that they re-elected him at their twelfth chapter, holden in London, 4th June, 1655."—MS. Notes of the late Canon Oliver, of Exeter.

1. His first work, published at Douay, in 1626, is entitled, *Tract. adversus Judiciarum Astrologiani.*

2. Then follows that to which in its reprint this sketch is prefixed:—*Paraphrastica Expositio Articulorum Confessionis Anglicæ.* This was first printed separately, but afterwards at the end of the *Tractatus de Prædestinatione, etc.* It was much "talked against" by the Jesuits, but having been formally sanctioned and approved at Rome, little was henceforth said about it. Though condemned in Spain † it was distinctly approved by several theologians and schools elsewhere, and was generally recognised by contemporary theologians.

3. *Tractatus de Prædestinatione, de Meritis et Peccatorum Remissione, etc.* Ludg. Bat. 1634. [Bodleian, A.A. 30. Th. Seld.] In the year following the said book came out with this title, *Deus, Natura, Gratia, sive Tractatus, etc.* [Lugduni, 1635. Bodleian, 8vo, C. 252.—British Museum, Lugduni, 1634, 4to. 4376. f.]

4. *Systema Fidei, sive Tractatus de Concilio Universali,* etc. Leod. 1648. [Bodleian. 4to. T. 79, Th.]

---

† "However in Spain it was censur'd, and how and why, let the author tell you in his own words (Letter dated 6th April, 1672), sent to me, thus:—'You told me that Mr. Leiburne shew'd you the *Index Expurgatorius* of Spain, wherein was named the Book of Articles published by me. There was here (in London) a Spanish ambassador *in the time of Oliver* ["under the rebels." First edition] named Alonzo de Cardenas, who had great malice to the last King, and being informed by a knave that the book was dedicated to, and accepted by, the King [Charles 1.] whom he esteemed his enemy, he surreptitiously procured in Spain to have it censured. He endeavoured to have it done so in Rome, but they answered as Pilate, '*Non invenio causam,*' and therefore it passed safe. This man (Alonzo) had been a Jesuit, and was esteemed not only to have left them rudely, but to have given himself up to get money, &c. In a letter also from Mr. Middleton (then chaplain to Basil, Lord Fielding, ambassador) to Archbishop Laud, dated at Venice, in December, 1635, I find there passages that the book of Sancta Clara, relished not well with the Catholics, and that there was a consultation about it, and some did '*extrema suadere,*' and cried '*ad ignem.*' Father Thomas Talbot, a Jesuit of Paris, told him so by letter, who, talking with the Pope's Nuncio at Paris about it, he told him it was the best course to let it die of itself, to which the Nuncio, a moderate man, was inclinable."—Wood's *Athenæ Oxoniensis.* Ed. Bliss. Vol. iii., p. 1224.

5. *Opusculum de Definabilitate Controversiæ Immaculatæ Conceptionis Dei Genitricis.* [Duaci, 1651, 4to. British Museum, 475, A. 6.]

6. *Tractatus de Schismate speciatim Anglicano.*

7. *Fragmenta: seu Historia minor provinciæ Angliæ Fratrum minorum.* [British Museum, 4to, 489½.]

8. *Manuale Missionariorum Regularium, præcipuè Anglorum S. Francisci,* etc. Printed at Douay, 1658, and again in 1661, in 12mo. [British Museum, 867, G. 2, and 866, A. 5.]

9. *Apologia Episcoporum,* etc. Colog. Agrip., 1640, 8vo. [Bodl., 8vo., c 4, Th. Seld.]

10. *Liber Dialogorum, seu Summa veteris Theologiæ Dialogismis tradita.* Duac., 1661, 8vo.

11. *Problemata Scholastica et Controversialia Speculativa,* etc.

12. *Collarium Dialogi de Medio Statu Animarum,* etc.

13. *Paralipomena Philosophica de Mundo Peripatetico.* This was published at Douay, under the name of Franciscus Coventriensis, in 1652, 8vo. [Bodleian, 8vo., c 41, Art. Seld.]; and at Antwerp, 1652, 8vo. [British Museum, 1135, B. 10.]

14. *Religio Philosophiæ peripatetici discutienda,* etc. Duaci, 1662, 8vo. [British Museum, 1019, D. 8.]

15. *Supplementum Historiæ provinciæ Angliæ,* etc. Duaci, 1671, fol.

16. *Disputatio de antiqua provinciæ præcedentia.* Duaci, 1671.

17. *Enchiridion of Faith,* etc. By Francis Coventrie. Douay, 1655, 12mo. [British Museum, 857, A. 22.]

18. *Explanation of the Roman Catholic Belief.* Printed 1656 [Bodleian, 8vo., c 716, Linc.]; reprinted 1670.

19. In addition to the above, a collected edition of his works (in two volumes) was issued, in 1665, from Douay—Duaci, typis Baltazaris Belleri, sub circeno aureo—[British Museum, 478, D. 12*] under the following title: *Operum Omnium Scholasticorum et Historicorum R. Adm. ac Eximii*

---

* Contains the author's autograph—"S. Angele, ex dono Authoris, 1670."

Patris Magistri F. Francisci a S. Clara. The contents of which are as follows: Vol. I.—(1.) **Systema Fidei.** (2.) *Tractatus de Schismate*, etc. (3.) *Fragmenta seu Historia FF. Minorum*, etc. (4.) *Manuale Missionariorum.* Vol. II.—(1.) *Apologia* **Episcoporum.** (2.) *Liber Dialogorum*, etc. (3.) *Problemata Scholastica.* (4.) *Opusculum de Medio Statu Animarum.* (5.) **Paralipomena** *Philosophica,* etc. (6.) *Religio Philosophiæ,* etc. (7.) *Epistola adversus Judiciarum Astrologiam.* [N.B. All these independent treatises are paged independently, and each is complete in itself, with its own title-page.]*

Sancta Clara, fortified by the Sacraments of Holy Church, died at the ripe age of eighty-two, at Somerset House, early in the morning, on the 31st of May, being Whitsun Monday, 1680, and was buried, not according to a wish expressed before his death, in a vault under the chapel of Somerset House, but in the Church of St. John, belonging to the Savoy Hospital in the Strand.† Antony à Wood remarks that Sancta Clara had previously wished especially to be interred in the Church of St. Ebbe in Oxford, to which an old house of the Franciscans formerly joined, and where several of his brethren of the order had been anciently laid to rest; but this desire, too, seems not to have been carried out. Thus passed away one, who, amid the trying scenes of a long lifetime, had striven patiently and charitably to bring together his fellow-countrymen into One religious obedience; and who, in the end, went to his account, doubtless, to receive in its fulness the blessed reward which the Peacemakers shall enjoy hereafter. F. G. L.

---

* In the Library of the Franciscan Convent at Taunton is preserved the MS. of Sancta Clara's translation from the Portuguese of the "*Chronicles of the Franciscan Order*," which was printed at St. Omer, in 4to, in 1618. [Qy? as to date. Ed.]

† In the MS. Franciscan Register it is said that " he accomplished three jubilees—of religion, of the priesthood, and of the mission: that to the end he proved himself a most loving father to his brethren and children, and a most watchful shepherd and faithful labourer in the English Mission during the space of fifty-seven years, making himself all to all to gain all to Christ."

The Rev. Henry White, M.A., chaplain of the Savoy Chapel, most courteously wrote to the editor, May 22, 1865, as follows:—" I have looked in vain for the register you seek—no such name appears at or about your date."

SERENISSIMO ATQUE INVICTISS. PRINCIPI

CAROLO I.

MAGNÆ BRITANNIÆ, &c., REGI.

SERENISSIME REX,

Scite dictum est illud Augustini contra Cresconium: Reges, in quantum Reges sunt, serviunt Deo, jubendo bona, et prohibendo mala, non solùm quæ pertinent ad humanam societatem, sed etiam quæ ad divinam Religionem. Non utique putatitio, nedum supposititio, sed plane reali titulo à Deo per Evangelicum Prophetam Isaiam ipsis concessum est; Erunt Reges nutritii tui, et Reginæ nutritiæ tuæ. Nutritiorum vero, sive tutorum est ἀρχιτεκτονικῶς mala pupillorum propulsare, bona præsertim, quæ ad pietatem spectant, viis sibi commodis promovere. Hinc Constantinus, animum in omnes, qui suberant imperio, intentum habuit, hortatus pro virili, ut piam omnes vitam excolerent. Ut olim notavit Eusebius in ejus vita lib. 4. Ad quam igitur, Serenissime Rex, in hac mira et misera corporis Christi dilaceratione recurrendum? nisi ad terram provolutus, sacram tuam Majestatem in opportunum Ecclesiæ sublevamen (cujus à Deo Nutritius, ab ejus Vicario Defensor constitutus sis) interpellem? Secundum illud Augustini ad Bonifacium: Cum

in angustiis affligitur Ecclesia, quisquis existimat, omnia potius sustinenda, quam Dei auxilium, ut per Imperatores Christianos feratur, esse poscendum, parum attendit, non bonam de hac negligentia reddi posse rationem.

Hilarium ergo, Constantinum in hunc modum alloquentem, miserias nostri sæculi (quibus succumbimus,) ipsiusmet verbis deplorans, insequar. Periculosum nobis admodum atque etiam miserabile est, tot nunc fides existere, quot voluntates: et tot nobis doctrinas esse, quot mores. Et postea: Dum aut ita fides scribuntur ut volumus, aut ut volumus intelliguntur.

Contremiscunt ossa mea dum hæc recogito; morbus, ubi spiritus vitales opprimuntur, nempe ut fides radix vitæ corrumpitur, difficillime sanatur. Hic morbus noster. Remedium tamen, et illud efficax, à Samaritano nostro designatum reperimus; nec aliud nisi illud: Dic Ecclesiæ. Dico. Ecclesiæ definitiones Majestati vestræ propono; Sanctorum Patrum et Venerabilium Doctorum expositiones, Novatorum ineptiis, præpono; quas dum modeste retego, in Christo tego, saniem, non scalpendo, sed suaviter lambendo lavo, ut abluam, sacro vestro Imperio opus, quippe ut executioni mandetur, quod ab Ecclesia et Sanctis Patribus sancitum est, secundum illud Justiniani Constit. 42: Hæc decrevimus, Sanctorum Patrum Canones secuti. Hoc tua Majestate dignum, hoc dignitati causæ consonum, hoc saluti animarum prorsus necessarium. Et omnis populus dicet, Amen.

Sacræ Suæ Majestatis

Devotissimus subditus,

Fr. Fran. a S. Clara.

CENSURÆ ET JUDICIA DOCTORUM.

Judicium eximii D. ac Magistri nostri Jacobi Dreux, Doctoris Sorbonici.

REVERENDE Pater. Summa cum animi voluptate, legi atque expendi partem utramque doctissimi tui Operis, in quo fateor, non modò me nihil deprehendisse à Fide orthodoxa bonisve moribus alienum, sed et laudasse consilium ac propositum tuum, quod in Ecclesiæ utilitatem cessurum auguror, ad conciliandos errantium animos, si Deus Opt. Max. cœptis tuis annuat; quod spero precorque. Ita me amare pergas, uti me ex animo profiteor

Tibi addictissimum

DREUX.

Londini pridie Calend. Augusti, 1633.

LIBRUM hunc inscriptum, *Deus, Natura, Gratia*, &c., vidi, legi, perlegi. Quid multa? Electione sententiarum, explicatione sacrarum Scripturarum et sanctorum Patrum, soliditate argumentorum, resolutionum pondere, claritate, methodo, stylo Scoto dignissimum reperi.

THOM. BLACLOUS,

S. Theol. Professor.

LIBELLUS qui sic inscribitur, *Articuli Confessionis Anglicanæ paraphrastice exponuntur*, &c., ex zelo Fidei et animarum scriptus omnibus

concordiæ et pacis Christianæ amicis non potest non esse acceptus, cum Catholico et animo et calamo scriptus sit, et errantibus, ut ad Christi caulam reditum inveniant, facem Catholicæ veritatis quasi ex propinquo ad alliciendos pusillanimes ostentet. Actum die 5 Julii, 1633.

Thom. Blaclous,
S. Theol. Professor.

PRO voto vestro amicus ille cujus judicium tanti facis, Librum hunc cui titulus, *Deus, Natura, et Gratia*, &c., perlegit, et dignum prælo censuit, sperans inter Protestantes saltem moderatiores, fructui futurum. Actum, 20 Aprilis.

Fr. Gul. Tomsonus,
S. Theol. Doctor.

AMICUS vester has ultimas chartas revisit, et idem de his quod de prioribus fert judicium. Actum, 22 Julii, 1633.

Fr. Gul. Tomsonus,
S. Theol. Doctor.

TRACTATUM hunc perlegi, et nihil contra Fidem Catholicam vel bonos mores aut ex alio titulo reprobandum : è contra vero doctrina Theologica et Scholastica subtiliter confertum, reperi. Et vere secundum calculum meum publicatio operis Protestantibus moderatioribus arridebit (omnibus placere difficillimum) et ad readunationem cum Ecclesia Romana, dum opportunum fuerit, disponet, et interim reverentiorem ejus æstimationem inuret. præsertim reliquos Confessionis Anglicæ Articulos (quod optarem) eadem moderatione exponere vellet, et ad calcem hujus operis (si pro voto successerit) Lectorem spe cæterorum, foveres. Hæc opinio mea, melius sententium judicio me submittens. Actum hac 16 April, 1633.

T. P. S. Theol. Professor.

(xxxv)

HANC posteriorem tractatus partem diligenter perlegi, et nihil non Catholicæ et Romanæ Fidei consentaneum reperi. Immo ut publicetur cum priori in commune bonum æque necessarium censeo: et quo citius, melius: publicatio enim operi expeditior non erit nociva, sed valde commoda. Actum hac 11 Julii, 1633.

Tho. P. S. Theol. Profess.

TENORE hujus testificor me sedulo perlegisse et accuratè recensuisse Librum inscriptum: *Deus, Natura, Gratia, cum tractatu de Meritis et peccatorum remissione, seu de Justificatione, denique de Sanctorum Invocatione, &c.* In quo nihil nisi Fidei orthodoxæ et Romanæ Ecclesiæ consentaneum occurrit: opus adeo dignissimum quod ad conscientiæ directionem, ingeniorum quantumvis subtilium eruditionem, et ad Reipubl. literariæ utilitatem typis commendetur, et in publicum quamprimum prodeat. Datum die 20 Junii, 1633.

Ægidius Chaissy, extra Mnr. Provinc. PP. Recol.
Prov. S. Bernardi, et olim tam in Italia, quam
Gallia, S. Theol. Lector Generalis.

HABITA ratione tui zeli et eruditionis, attentis etiam testimoniis horum in Schola Theologica per illustrium virorum, Facultatem facio, quatenus, cum salutaris obedientiæ merito, tractatum de justificatione et problematibus annexis præ lo mandare, ut poteris citius, cures. Vale, Deum pro nobis oraturus.

Fr. Joan. Gennings,
Angliæ Mnr.

PLACET, ut hæc Expositio paraphrastica, testimonio tantorum virorum approbata prælo mandetur. Hac 20 Julii, 1633.

Fr. Joan. Gennings.

VIDI et attente perlegi utramque partem hujus operis, cui prior titulus, *Deus, Natura, Gratia*, &c., posterior, *Articuli Confessionis Anglicanae paraphrastice exponuntur*, &c. In quo universa comperi, non solum verae fidei et orthodoxae religioni, necnon optimis moribus consona, sed etiam mira pietate ac eruditione referta, dignumque censui qui possit typis mandari, in cujus rei fidem hoc propria manu scripsi et subscripsi. Actum die 24 Aug. 1633.

        PETRUS MARTINUS,
            Theol. Professor.

OMNIA haec superius exscripta exempla vidi, et cum singulis eorum Originalibus contuli, quibuscum ea concordare testor infra scriptus.

Datum Londini, 30 Calend. Septembr. 1633.

D.D.M.C.   D. DAVID, Monachus et Decanus Congregationis
Fidelis.   Casinensis olim Romae Sereniss. D. N. Urbani
        Papae octavi Poenitentiarius, **Notarius Apostolicus**.

ARTICULI

CONFESSIONIS ANGLICÆ,

PARAPHRASTICE EXPONUNTUR,

ET IN QUANTUM CUM VERITATE COMPOSSIBILES REDDI POSSUNT, PERLUSTRANTUR.

ARTICULUS I.—*De Fide in Sacrosanctam Trinitatem.*

UNUS est vivus et verus Deus, æternus, incorporeus, impartibilis, impassibilis, immensæ potentiæ, sapientiæ, ac bonitatis, Creator atque Conservator omnium, tum visibilium, tum invisibilium. Et in unitate hujus divinæ naturæ, tres sunt personæ, ejusdem essentiæ, potentiæ, ac æternitatis, Pater, Filius, et Spiritus Sanctus.

ARTICULUS II.—*De Verbo, sive Filio Dei, qui verus Homo factus est.*

FILIUS, qui est Verbum Patris, ab æterno a Patre genitus, verus et æternus Deus, ac Patri consubstantialis, in utero Beatæ Virginis, ex illius substantia, naturam humanam assumpsit: ita ut duæ naturæ divina et humana, integre atque perfecte in unitate personæ fuerint

THE ARTICLES

OF THE

ANGLICAN CONFESSION

PARAPHRASTICALLY EXPLAINED,

AND CONSIDERED AS TO HOW FAR THEY CAN BE RECONCILED WITH THE TRUE FAITH.

ARTICLE I.—*Of Faith in the Holy Trinity.*

THERE is but one living and true God, everlasting, without body, parts, or passions; of infinite power, wisdom, and goodness; the Maker, and Preserver of all things both visible and invisible. And in unity of this Godhead there be three Persons, of one substance, power, and eternity; the Father, the Son, and the Holy Ghost.

ARTICLE II.—*Of the Word or Son of God, which was made very Man.*

THE Son, which is the Word of the Father, begotten from everlasting of the Father, the very and eternal God, and of one substance with the Father, took Man's nature in the womb of the blessed Virgin, of her substance: so that two whole and perfect Natures, that is to say,

inseparabiliter conjunctæ, ex quibus est unus Christus, verus Deus et verus homo, qui vere passus est, crucifixus, mortuus, et sepultus, ut Patrem nobis reconciliaret, essetque hostia, non tantum pro culpa originis, verum etiam pro omnibus actualibus hominum peccatis.

ARTICULUS III.—*De descensu Christi ad Inferos.*

QUEMADMODUM Christus pro nobis mortuus est, et sepultus, ita est etiam credendus ad Inferos descendisse.

ARTICULUS IV.—*De Resurrectione Christi.*

CHRISTUS vere a mortuis resurrexit, suumque corpus cum carne, ossibus, omnibusque ad integritatem humanæ naturæ pertinentibus, recepit; cum quibus in cœlum ascendit, ibique residet, quoad extremo die ad judicandos homines reversurus sit.

ARTICULUS V.—*De Spiritu Sancto.*

SPIRITUS Sanctus, a Patre et Filio procedens, ejusdem est cum Patre et Filio essentiæ, majestatis, et gloriæ, verus ac æternus Deus.

the Godhead and Manhood, were joined together in one Person, never to be divided, whereof is one Christ, very God, and very Man; who truly suffered, was crucified, dead and buried, to reconcile his Father to us, and to be a sacrifice, not only for original guilt, but also for all actual sins of men.

ARTICLE III.—*Of the going down of Christ into Hell.*

AS Christ died for us, and was buried, so also is it to be believed, that he went down into Hell.

ARTICLE IV.—*Of the Resurrection of Christ.*

CHRIST did truly rise again from death, and took again his body, with flesh, bones, and all things appertaining to the perfection of Man's nature; wherewith he ascended into Heaven, and there sitteth, until he return to judge all Men at the last day.

ARTICLE V.—*Of the Holy Ghost.*

THE Holy Ghost, proceeding from the Father and the Son, is of one substance, majesty, and glory, with the Father and the Son, very and eternal God.

ARTICULUS VI.—*De divinis Scripturis, quod sufficiant ad salutem.*

SCRIPTURA sacra continet omnia, quæ ad salutem sunt necessaria, ita ut quicquid in ea nec legitur, neque inde probari potest, non sit a quoquam exigendum, ut tanquam articulus fidei credatur, aut ad salutis necessitatem requiri putetur. Sacræ Scripturæ nomine, eos canonicos libros Veteris et Novi Testamenti intelligimus, de quorum auctoritate in Ecclesia nunquam dubitatum est.

PARAPHRASIS.—Quinque Articuli priores solum Symbolum Apostolorum exponunt, nec ministrant materiam examinis. Articulus vero sextus quoad priorem paragraphum examinabitur in Articulis 20, 21, et 34.

ARTICLE VI.— *Of the Sufficiency of the holy Scriptures for Salvation.*

HOLY Scripture containeth all things necessary to salvation: so that whatsoever is not read therein, nor may be proved thereby,* is not to be required of any man, that it should be believed as an article of the Faith, or be thought requisite or necessary to salvation. In the name of the Holy Scripture we do understand those Canonical Books of the Old and New Testament, of whose authority was never any doubt in the Church.†

EXPLANATION. — The first five Articles merely explain the Apostles' Creed, and afford no matter for examination. The sixth Article, however, as respects the first paragraph, will be examined in treating of Ar-

---

* [Vide Article XX., which supplies what is wanting here. "May be proved thereby,"—*i.e.*, by the (Catholic or Universal) Church. For "the Church .... hath authority in controversies of Faith."]

† [By the same rule by which this Article is made to exclude the so-called "Apocrypha," must be excluded—if the rule be faithfully and impartially applied—The Book of Revelations, St. Paul's Epistle to the Hebrews, and The Second Epistle of St. Peter, besides important portions of other parts of the New Testament. The Third and Fourth Books of Esdras, and The Prayer of Manasses, were not received by the Council of Trent. Baruch the Prophet, The Song of the Three Children (*Benedicite*), The Story of Susanna, and The Book of Bel and the Dragon, were frequently quoted by the Fathers as portions respectively of Jeremiah and Daniel. It should be further remarked that this Article does not declare the "other books" —commonly called the "Apocrypha"—to be (A) either destitute of inspiration, or (B) simply human; but only declares that (the Church) "doth not apply them to establish any doctrine."]

Quod verò subdit de numero Scripturarum Canonicarum, hujus loci est.

*De nominibus et numero Librorum Sacræ Scripturæ Canonicæ veteris Testamenti.**

Genesis, Exodus, Leviticus, Numeri, Deuteron: prior Liber Paralipomenôn, primus Liber Esdræ, secundus Liber Esdræ, Liber Esther, Josue, Judicum, Ruth, prior Liber Regum, Secundus Liber Regum, prior Liber Samuelis, Secundus Liber Samuelis, Liber Job, Psalmi, Proverbia, Ecclesiastes vel Concionator, Cantica Solomonis, quatuor Prophetæ majores, duodecim Prophetæ minores.

Cæteros, authoritate Hieronymi, adducti in Ecclesiis ad mores instruendos, non ad doctrinam firmandam legi jubent. Cujus generis sunt :—

ticles 20, 21, and 34; but the remainder, concerning the number of the Books of Canonical Scripture, belongs to this place.

Of the names and number of the Books of Canonical Scripture of the Old Testament.

Genesis, Exodus, Leviticus, **Numbers**, Deuteronomy, Joshua, Judges, Ruth, The First Book of Samuel, The Second Book of Samuel, The First Book of Kings, The Second Book of Kings, The First **Book** of Chronicles, The Second Book of Chronicles, The First Book of Esdras, The Second Book of Esdras, The Book of Esther, The Book of Job, The Psalms, **The** Proverbs, Ecclesiastes or the Preacher, **Cantica**, or Songs of Solomon, Four Prophets the greater, Twelve Prophets the less.

The remaining books, on the authority of Jerome, they order to be read in Church for instruction of manners, not for the establishing of doctrine, of which kind are:—

---

* [This part of Article VI., reprinted *verbatim* from the edition of Sancta Clara, published in London, without any printer's name, A.D. 1646, is not, as far as its actual text is concerned, quite accurate in the order in which the Old Testament Books are placed. The paragraph above, beginning "Cæteros, etc.," stands as follows in the Latin edition of Kay:—" Alios autem Libros (ut ait Hieronymus) legit quidem Ecclesia, ad exempla vitæ, et formandos mores: illos tamen ad dogmata confirmanda non adhibet, ut sunt :—" and thus in the English form of the Article :— " And the other books (as *Hierome* saith) the Church doth read for example of life and instruction of manners; but yet doth it not apply them to establish any doctrine ; such as these following :—."]

Tertius Liber Esdræ, **quartus Liber Esdræ, Liber Tobiæ, Liber Judith,** reliquum Libri Esther, Liber Sapientiæ, Liber Jesu filii Sirach, Baruch Prophetæ, Canticum trium puerorum, Historiæ Susannæ, de Bel et Dracone, Oratio Manasses, prior Liber Maccabæorum, **secundus Liber Maccabæorum.**

Novi Testamenti omnes Libros (ut vulgò recepti sunt) recipimus et habemus pro Canonicis.

PARAPHRASIS.—Inter Catholicos, paucissimos invenio viros eruditos, qui post Florentinum, **in** dubium vocarunt ullos ex Libris **ibi pro** Canonicis declaratis, nisi Cajetanum in fine suorum Commentariorum **super** Libros historiarum Veteris Testamenti, qui Libros in Articulo exceptos, Canonicos rectè appellari fatetur ob authoritatem Conciliorum et aliquorum Patrum, sed in dissimili gradu; scilicet, ut hic in Articulo: *non ad Fidem firmandam, sed solùm ad mores instruendos;* ut olim loquutus est **Ruffinus** in Expositione **Symboli. Franciscus** etiam Mirandula "De Fide et ordine Credendi" idem planè asserit ex Hieronymo, et

The Third Book of Esdras, The Fourth Book of Esdras, The Book of Tobias, The Book of Judith, The rest **of** the **Book of** Esther, The **Book of Wisdom, Jesus** the Son of Sirach, Baruch the Prophet, The **Song** of the Three Children, **The Story of** Susanna, Of Bel and the **Dragon, The** Prayer of Manasses, **The First Book of** Maccabees, The **Second Book of** Maccabees.

All the Books of **the New Testa**ment, as they are commonly received, we do receive, and account them Canonical.

EXPLANATION.— Among Catholics, **I** find very few learned men who since the Council of Florence have raised a doubt concerning any of the Books there declared Canonical, except Cajetan, at the end of his Commentaries on the Historical Books of the Old Testament. He confesses that the Books excepted in **the Arti**cle are rightly called "Canonical," on account of the authority of Councils and some Fathers; but in a different degree, as here in the Article, *not for the establishing of the Faith, but only for instruction of manners;* as was said long since by Ruffinus in his "Exposition of the Creed." Franciscus Mirandula, too, in his treatise

ad eundem fere sensum citat S. Antoninum, post Lyranum in præfatione ad libros **Tobiæ**.

Hæc eorum opinio, licet singularis valde et certe hæresi proxima est, præsertim post Trid. ubi illos in Canonem reponi declarat, secundum quod ante fecerat Florentinum cum consensu utriusque Ecclesiæ.

Saltem sic Charanza citat Florentinum, et alii ipso seniores. Video tamen ab aliis viris doctis in dubium verti, an Florentinum libros illos hodie controversos, ut Canonicos declaraverit: sed de Trid. constat. Quia tamen Articulus non omnino rejicit eos ex Canone, non videtur esse hæresim simpliciter: sic etiam Melchior Cano in locis l. 2. c. 9. ubi tamen fatetur *esse hæresi proximam, quia certe veritati Catholicæ fidei adversatur; non manifeste quidem, sed sapientum omnium longe probabili ac ferme necessariæ sententiæ.* Facile enim esset hujus modi glossemate, quascunque quorumcunque Concili-

"De fide et ordine Credendi," makes the same plain assertion from St. Jerome, and cites St. Antoninus to almost the same purport, after De Lyra in the "Preface to the Books of Tobias."

Such is their opinion, though it be quite singular and certainly approximating to heresy, especially since the Council of Trent, which places the Books in the Canon in accordance with what the Council of Florence, with the consent of both Churches, Eastern and Western, had previously done.

At least Charanza and others before him cite the Council of Florence to this purport. I find, however, that other learned men raise a a doubt as to whether the Council of Florence declared the Books, which are at present controverted, to be Canonical; but it is agreed that Trent did. Since, however, the Article does not wholly reject them from the Canon, it does not seem to be heresy, absolutely. According to Melchior Cano, in his "Loci Theologici" (bk. ii. c. 9), where, however, he allows it "*to approximate to heresy, because it is certainly repugnant to the truth of the Catholic Faith: not openly*

orum definitiones eludere et evertere. Scio tamen Waldensem, l. 2, Doctrinalis Fidei Antiq. c. 19. tenere quod authoritas declarandi et approbandi sacros libros sit in serie Patrum omnium, et fidelium ab Apostolis succedentium: sic etiam Driedonis l. i. De Eccles. Scripturis et Dogmatibus, c. i. et hinc minus ausim sententiam prætactam Cajetani, et hujus Articuli hæreseos insimulare.

indeed; but by being opposed to the very probable and almost necessary opinion of all learned men." For it would be easy, by a gloss of this kind, to escape from and overthrow any definitions of any Councils. I know however that Waldensis, "Doctr. Fid. Antiq." (bk. ii. c. 19), holds that the authority for declaring and approving the Sacred Books rests with the series of all the Fathers and faithful in succession from the Apostles, with whom agrees Driedonis "De Eccles. Script. et Dogm." (bk. i. c. i.)—for these reasons, I should the rather shrink from charging heresy upon the above-mentioned opinion of Cajetan and upon this Article.

ARTICULUS VII.—*De Veteri Testamento.*

TESTAMENTUM Vetus Novo contrarium non est, quandoquidem tam in Veteri, quam in Novo per Christum, qui unicus est Mediator, Dei et hominum, Deus et homo, æterna vita humano generi est proposita. Quare male sentiunt, qui veteres tantum in promissiones temporarias sperasse confingunt. Quanquam lex a Deo data per Mosen (quoad cæremonias et ritus) Christianos non astringat, neque civilia

ARTICLE VII.—*Of the Old Testament.*

THE Old Testament is not contrary to the New: for both in the Old and New Testament everlasting life is offered to Mankind by Christ, who is the only Mediator between God and Man, being both God and Man. Wherefore they are not to be heard, which feign that the old Fathers did look only for transitory promises. Although the Law given from God by Moses, as touching Ceremonies and Rites, do not bind

ejus præcepta in aliqua republica necessario recipi debeant; nihilominus tamen ab obedientia mandatorum (quæ moralia vocantur) nullus (quantumvis Christianus) est solutus.

PARAPHRASIS.—Hic Articulus per totum Catholicus est.

ARTICULUS VIII.—*De tribus Symbolis.*

SYMBOLA tria Nicænum, Athanasii, et quod vulgo Apostolorum appellatur, omnino recipienda sunt et credenda; nam firmissimis Scripturarum testimoniis probari possunt.

PARAPHRASIS.—De hoc idem est judicium.

ARTICULUS IX.—*De Peccato Originali.*

PECCATUM originis non est (ut fabulantur Pelagiani) in imitatione Adami situm, sed est vitium, et depravatio naturæ, cujuslibet hominis ex Adamo naturaliter propagati: qua fit, ut ab originali justitia quam longissime distet; ad malum sua natura propendeat; et caro semper adversus spiritum concupiscat;

Christian men, nor the Civil precepts thereof ought of necessity to be received in any common-wealth; yet notwithstanding, no Christian man whatsoever is free from the obedience of the Commandments which are called Moral.

EXPLANATION.—This Article is Catholic throughout.

ARTICLE VIII.—*Of the Three Creeds.*

THE Three Creeds, *Nicene* Creed, *Athanasius's* Creed, and that which is commonly called the *Apostles'* Creed, ought thoroughly to be received and believed; for they may be proved by most certain warrants of holy Scripture.

EXPLANATION. — The judgment upon this is the same.

ARTICLE IX.—*Of Original or Birth-sin.*

ORIGINAL Sin standeth not in the following of *Adam*, as the *Pelagians* do vainly talk; but it is the fault and corruption of the Nature of every man, that naturally is ingendered of the offspring of *Adam*; whereby man is very far gone from original righteousness, and is of his own nature inclined to evil, so that

unde in unoquoque nascentium, iram Dei atque damnationem meretur. Manet etiam in renatis hæc naturæ depravatio : qua fit, ut affectus carnis, Græce φρόνημα σαρκὸς (quod alii sapientiam, alii sensum, alii affectum, alii studium carnis interpretantur), legi Dei non subjiciatur. Et quanquam renatis et credentibus nulla propter Christum est condemnatio, peccati tamen in sese rationem habere concupiscentiam, fatetur Apostolus.

the flesh lusteth always contrary to the spirit; and therefore in every person born into this world, it deserveth God's wrath and damnation. And this infection of nature doth remain, yea in them that are regenerated; whereby the lust of the flesh, called in Greek, *phronema sarkos*, which some do expound the wisdom, some sensuality, some the affection, some the desire, of the flesh, is not subject to the Law of God. And although there is no condemnation for them that believe and are baptized, yet the Apostle doth confess, that concupiscence and lust hath of itself the nature of sin.

PARAPHRASIS.—Prior pars sanam continet doctrinam, et tam sanctis Patribus, quam Theologis valde conformem. Posterior vero, quæ incipit: *manet etiam in renatis*, examinatur prope finem Problematis 12.

EXPLANATION.—The former part of this Article contains sound doctrine, entirely in agreement both with the holy Fathers and with Theologians. The latter part, however, commencing, "And this infection" is examined towards the end of Problem 12.

EXPLANATION FROM PROBLEM XII.—With respect to what is said in Article IX., that "concupiscence hath of itself the nature of sin," it would seem somewhat difficult to explain this, unless the Article had said before how this should be understood, in these words, "This sensuality, affection, or desire of the flesh, is not subject to the law of God." It is, therefore, said to have of itself the nature of sin, because it is not subject to the divine law, and no more. It has not, therefore, formally the nature of sin, but only by way of disposition, because in truth it disposes or inclines us

against the law of God: undoubtedly, then, it has no other meaning than that which, in a former quotation, St. Augustine gave to the words of St. Paul—that is, that it has the nature of sin, because it is from sin and leads to sin. (*S. Aug. "Cont. Ep. Pelag."* l. i., c. 13, explaining Col. iii. 5.)

It is said, too, in the Article, to be not subject to the divine law; because it raises contests, which are sometimes severe, between the flesh and the spirit, which St. Paul describes in his Ep. to the Galatians (v. 17); and for this cause is called by many of the ancients "the tyrant in our members;" by others, "the weakness of our nature;" by St. Paul, "the law of the members," and, by Augustine, "the law of the flesh;" which epithets, though they do not imply what is formally sin, yet plainly suggest in some manner the nature of sin, or lack of subordination to the divine law, which is quite sufficient to agree with the Article.

ARTICULUS X.—*De Libero Arbitrio.*

EA est hominis post lapsum Adæ conditio, ut sese naturalibus suis viribus, et bonis operibus, ad fidem et invocationem Dei convertere, ac præparare non possit: Quare absque gratia Dei (quæ per Christum est) nos præveniente, ut velimus, et cooperante, dum volumus, ad pietatis opera facienda, quæ Deo grata sunt et accepta, nihil valemus.

ARTICLE X.—*Of Free-Will.*

THE condition of Man after the fall of *Adam* is such, that he cannot turn and prepare himself, by his own natural strength and good works, to faith, and calling upon God: Wherefore we have no power to do good works pleasant and acceptable to God, without the grace of God by Christ preventing us, that we may have a good will, and working with us, when we have that good will.

PARAPHRASIS.—Catholicus est, et declaratur Problematibus 10, 11, 12, immo à Prob. 5 ad 12.

EXPLANATION.—This Article is Catholic, and is explained in Problems 10, 11, 12; or, indeed, from Problems 5 to 12.

EXPLANATION FROM PROBLEM XI.—This is entirely true throughout, and in conformity with the Councils of Orange, Milevis, and Trent, as is

abundantly clear from former quotations, and others to be considered hereafter.

First is the decision of Orange (ii. § 3).—"If any man say that grace can be gained by man's own calling upon God, and not that grace itself leads us to call for it, he contradicts the Prophet Isaiah (lxv. 1), and the Apostle using the same words (Romans x. 21). 'I was found of them that sought me not. I was made manifest unto them that asked not after me.'"

Secondly (§ 7).—"If any one should say that we, of our own natural strength, think, or choose—that is, will, &c., any good thing which pertains to our eternal salvation, without the illumination and inspiration of the Holy Spirit: he is deceived by an heretical spirit, not understanding the word of God in the Gospel—'Without Me ye can do nothing;' and that saying of the Apostle, 'Not that we are sufficient of ourselves to think anything as of ourselves, but our sufficiency is of God.'" And in all points the doctrine of the Tridentine Council is the same.

There is not a word, as may here be seen, against the power of Free Will in order to moral acts. And this can be confirmed by the authority of many Protestant Doctors: for instance, Dr. Whittaker, "*De peccato origin.*" (ii. 3), says as follows:—"If, by a moral act, you mean the Philosophical Virtues, we do not deny that a man, without special grace may act in many things with fortitude, temperance, and justice." These are his words. He used the words "Philosophical Virtues," that he might exclude virtues conducing to salvation, which is our very doctrine. Montagu also, "*Appellat.*" (c. x.), at length, both in his own name and in that of others, treats of and defends this truth.

Articulus XI.—*De Hominis Justificatione.*

TANTUM propter meritum Domini ac Salvatoris nostri Jesu Christi per Fidem, non propter opera et merita nostra, justi coram Deo reputamur. Quare sola fide nos justificari doctrina est saluberrima ac consolationis plenissima, ut in Homilia

Article XI.—*Of the Justification of Man.*

WE are accounted righteous before God, only for the merit of our Lord and Saviour Jesus Christ by Faith, and not for our own works or deservings: Wherefore, that we are justified by Faith only is a most wholesome Doctrine, and very

de Justificatione hominis fusius explicatur.	full of comfort, as more largely is expressed in the Homily of Justification.*
PARAPHRASIS.—Hic Articulus examinatur fuse Probl. 22.	EXPLANATION.—This article is examined at length in Problem 22.

EXPLANATION FROM PROBLEM XXII.—To speak truly, I think that this whole question, between Protestants and ourselves, has fallen through, unless we wish to amuse ourselves with words; for there never was a question concerning the efficient cause of justification; because, as I said, this God alone is according to the belief of all; nor again concerning the meritorious cause, which, as I have also said, is Christ alone, or His passion; nor concerning the material cause, for to that is subject to that which is said to be justified—namely, man; as a wall in respect of whiteness; nor concerning the final cause, for the end of all the Predestined is Christ, as in Ephesians I.—" Having predestinated us by Jesus Christ to himself."

If, then, there be any difficulty, it concerns the formal cause; but neither do Protestants attribute this to faith; for this is expressly declared in the Book of Homilies (as it is called amongst Anglicans, with whom it is a great authority).

So, then, it will be plain that, under neither of the heads of causation, is our justification attributed to faith; and indeed, according to them, we are to no extent justified by faith, unless you would say by faith as a foundation, or as a condition or disposition; which we, too, have said in treating of merit, and have proved from St. Augustine, and as is defined by the Council of Trent (Sess. vi. c. 7).

But, if you would say that justification is acquired by faith, as applying or laying hold of the merits or righteousness of Christ, I think that this may bear a sound and Catholic sense; because, in truth, we by faith (according to the text, "He that cometh to God must believe that He is"), trusting to the promises of God in Christ, or to the merits of Christ's

---

* [There is no Homily—either in the Book published in the reign of Edward the VIth, nor in that of which a Table of Contents is given in Article XXXV., entitled, a "Homily of Justification."]

sufferings, by prayer, by charity, &c., at length obtain through Christ our justification.

This is their doctrine, and ours too; nor do they attribute more to faith as regards justification, than does the Council of Trent, if they are explained with caution—that is, in the manner just mentioned; but the difference really is as to what is to be understood by "Faith." They think that it means a leaning on, or act of confidence in, the promises of God; while we think this to be the same thing with that faith of Christ, preached to the nations everywhere, by which we believe all the promises of God; (unless one may say more correctly, as above, that this rather belongs to hope) : here, then, we might very easily come to an agreement, for in this manner does Montagu rightly explain the article " *De fide*."

Indeed, they themselves [the Anglicans] attribute the effect, not to that special faith, but to the faith of Christ, as we do, for in the Articles no faith is specified, but that of which the Apostles always speak. As regards this point then there is no disagreement.*

NOTE FROM PROBLEM XXVI.—God on account of Christ's righteousness imputed to us, as if on account of a meritorious cause, grants us our righteousness [*i. e.* "inherent righteousness"]. All which being duly weighed, in reality no discrepancy can now be found between the Anglican Confession and the Tridentine definition; nor does anything in the Hampton Court Articles make for the contrary opinion, as is clear from Article IX. on Justification; whence Montagu, in his "*Appello Cæsarem*" (c. 6), expressly proves that our doctrine at least, with this latitude, is held by them, and in the same passage quotes Dr. White, who asserts that in the justification of the sinner there are two actions on the part of God—one whereby He remits the sin; the other whereby He gives the man power to resist sin, which power is love infused into our hearts by that second act of God; which is identical with our doctrine. On this point, too, therefore, there is agreement.

---

* [" A number of means go to effect our justification. We are justified by Christ alone, in that He has purchased the gift; by Faith alone, in that Faith asks for it; by Baptism alone, for Baptism conveys it; and by newness of heart alone, for newness of heart is the life of it." Tract 90, 3rd Edit., p. 13.]

Articulus XII.—De bonis Operibus.

BONA opera quæ sunt fructus Fidei et justificatos sequuntur, quamquam peccata nostra expiare et divini judicii severitatem ferre non possunt; Deo tamen grata sunt, et accepta in Christo, atque ex vera et viva Fide, necessariò profluunt, ut planè ex illis æquè Fides viva cognosci possit, atque arbor ex fructu judicari.

Article XII.—Of Good Works.

ALBEIT that Good Works, which are the fruits of Faith, and follow after Justification, cannot put away our sins, and endure the severity of God's Judgment; yet are they pleasing and acceptable to God in Christ, and do spring out necessarily of a true and lively Faith; insomuch that by them a lively Faith may be as evidently known as a tree discerned by the fruit.

EXPLANATION FROM PROBLEM XXI.—With respect to what we have said that, after justification, we can merit an increase of righteousness and glory, the twelfth Article is clearly on our side, which is in the following words—"Albeit that good works," &c.

What is the meaning of "acceptable to God in Christ," except that through Christ they are accepted, so as to be rewarded; or, that by force of the divine and eternal promise, made to us through Christ, they are meritorious, &c.; which is the doctrine of the Subtle Doctor, and that commonly received at present?

But what is said in the previous words, that they "cannot put away our sins, and endure the severity of God's judgment," must be explained by accommodating these statements to what we have just said—that is, they cannot do so except *in Christ*, as is clearly expressed in the latter part of the Article. For nothing is of any value, speaking strictly, *if Christ be excluded*. In this sense, too, is said above, "nor endure the severity of God's judgment;" not that they will be punished, but that they will not be rewarded, because with respect to reward they *have no value* without Christ, as we all allow. With respect to this, then, we are in agreement.

Articulus XIII.—De operibus ante Justificationem.

OPERA quæ fiunt ante gratiam Christi, et Spiritus ejus afflatum,

Article XIII.—Of Works before Justification.

WORKS done before the grace of Christ, and the Inspiration of

cum ex fide Jesu Christi non prodeant, minime Deo grata sunt, neque gratiam (ut multum vocant) de congruo merentur. Immo, cum non sunt facta ut Deus illa fieri voluit et præcepit, peccati rationem habere non dubitamus.

his Spirit, are not pleasant to God, forasmuch as they spring not of faith in Jesus Christ, neither do they make men meet to receive grace, or (as the School-authors say) deserve grace of congruity: yea, rather, for that they are not done as God hath willed and commanded them to be done, we doubt not but they have the nature of sin.

PARAPHRASIS.—Examinatur hic Artic. Problematibus 18, 20, 21.

EXPLANATION.—This Article is examined in Problems 18, 20, 21.

EXPLANATION FROM PROBLEM XXI.—In these words it is evident that the only works excluded from merit of congruity with respect to our justification, are works done before faith in Christ—that is, before the first actual grace, or inspiration of the Holy Spirit (as is said in the same Article). Since, then, "the exception proves the rule" as lawyers say, it follows that other works—namely, those done in faith—can dispose us in some degree for justification, and deserve, of congruity *(de congruo)*, the grace of justification, which is the opinion of St. Augustine; which, perhaps, the compilers had in their mind, and so far most rightly. (See Note from Prob. XXI. *inf.* p. 16.)

But, with respect to what is added, that "such works have rather the nature of sin," we must first notice that they are not said absolutely to be sins, but rather to "partake of the nature of sin," which, undoubtedly, is a term of diminution (as the Summulists* say); else, they would rather unreservedly have been called *sins*. The meaning is that, by taking sin in a wide sense, or extending the nature of sin, such works can be brought under it—that is, inasmuch as they are not done in conformity with the laws of God; as is clearly expressed in these words—"For that they are not done as God hath willed and commanded them to be done." For that a thing is done not as God has ordered, or not in conformity with the Divine Will as revealed in His laws, is not at once assumed to be sin speaking positively, but only negatively: otherwise, that a work should be done not in conformity with the law would be the same as if it were in positive disa-

---

* ["Ut loquuntur Summulistæ." Ed. Lugduni, 1634; ed. Londini, 1646.]

greement with it, which alone is, strictly speaking, sin; and further, that all indifferent acts would be sins, which is absurd: yet, they are not done in conformity with the law, for then they would be good, not indifferent. The intention then is to call the works in question *sins*, improperly; or according to the schools, negatively. And, in truth, this is the very doctrine of the Council of Orange, and of St. Augustine especially (lib. iii., *Cont. Ep. Pelag.*, c. 5)—"The just man lives by faith; for, without it, even what seem to be good works, are turned into sin." And he proves it from St. Paul, "Whatsoever is not of faith is sin." And this is the common doctrine of the schoolmen.

NOTE FROM PROBLEM XXI.—St. Aug., Ep. 105.—"Nor does remission of sins itself take place without some merit—forsooth, faith obtains this; for faith is not devoid of merit, by which faith the publican said, 'God be merciful to me a sinner,' and went down to his house justified, being humbled by merit of faith. It remains, then, that we must not attribute faith itself to the human will in which they are puffed up (the Semi-pelagians); nor to any preceding merits (for whatever good acts are meritorious have their origin from faith); but we must confess it to be the free gift of God, if we think of true grace, that is, without merit." What can be more clear, he says, that, through faith, grace of justification is merited, but not of condignity; so that it must be of congruity.

ARTICULUS XIV.—*De Operibus Supererogationis.*

OPERA quæ supererogationis appellant, non possunt sine arrogantia et impietate prædicari. Nam illis declarant homines, non tantum se Deo reddere, quæ tenentur: sed plus in Ejus gratiam facere quam deberent; cum aperte Christus dicat, Cum feceritis omnia quæcunque præcepta sunt vobis, dicite, Servi inutiles sumus.

ARTICLE XIV.—*Of Works of Supererogation.*

VOLUNTARY Works, besides, over and above, God's Commandments, which they call Works of Supererogation, cannot be taught without arrogancy and impiety: for by them men do declare, that they do not only render unto God as much as they are bound to do, but that they do more for His sake, than of bounden duty is required: whereas Christ saith plainly, When ye have done all that are commanded to you, say, We are unprofitable servants.

PARAPHRASIS. — Examinatur hic Artic. Problemate 36.	EXPLANATION. — This Article is examined in Problem 36.

EXPLANATION FROM PROBLEM XXXVI.—To speak the truth, the explanation of this Article would seem somewhat hard, did not the latter part diminish the difficulty. For Works of Supererogation are so far condemned as, by them, men declare that they render more to God than they are bound to do on any ground. For those words placed without limitation ("They render more than they are bound to do"), according to the rules of the schools, are to be interpreted universally; and then the sense will be, "They render more than they are bound to do, in any manner, or by any just claim." Such works, then, the Article condemns; and so, too, do we. Moreover, did God exact all that He might justly claim and we owe, we should be wholly unprofitable and most miserable: we owe everything to Him, for there is nothing which we have not received. We do not, therefore, boast that we render more to God than we are bound to do, if we include every kind of debt.

Moreover, the Article speaks of the Works of a man in a state of pure nature—that is, not prevented nor assisted by God's grace; which is evident from the fact that it does not once mention *grace*, while we speak of man in a state of righteousness, that is, furnished with the grace of God.

In this, then, there is nothing against the doctrine of Works of Supererogation proved by us from the Fathers, and supported also by their own authorities of most weight. Some Calvinists calumniate us by alleging certain frivolous and untrue statements with respect to this point of Supererogation. May God forgive them for deceitfully ensnaring souls, otherwise well affected towards the truth! Meanwhile, on our side are both the Anglican Articles, and those who follow them without guile.

ARTICULUS XV.—*De Christo, Qui solus est sine peccato.*	ARTICLE XV.—*Of Christ alone without Sin.*
CHRISTUS in nostræ naturæ veritate, per omnia similis factus est nobis, excepto peccato, a quo prorsus erat immunis, tum in carne, tum in spiritu. Venit ut Agnus absque	CHRIST in the truth of our nature was made like unto us in all things, sin only except, from which He was clearly void, both in His flesh, and in His spirit. He came to be the

macula, Qui mundi peccata per immolationem Sui semel factam tolleret; et peccatum (ut inquit Johannes) in Eo non erat: sed nos reliqui, etiam baptizati, et in Christo regenerati, in multis tamen offendimus omnes. Et si dixerimus, quia peccatum non habemus, nos ipsos seducimus, et veritas in nobis non est.

PARAPHRASIS. — Hic Articulus usque ad hæc verba: *Sed nos reliqui etiam baptizati*, etc. sanctissimus est: ibi vero indiget glossa, non mea, sed magni Augustini in l. de Natura et Gra. contra Pelagianos:—

"*Cum de peccatis agitur, de S. Virgine Maria propter* honorem Domini nullam prorsus habere volo quæstionem, inde enim scimus, quod ei plus gratiæ collatum fuerit ad vincendum omni ex parte peccatum, quod concipere ac parere meruit eum, quem constat nullum habuisse peccatum. Hæc ergo Virgine excepta, si omnes illos Sanctos et Sanctas, qui in Scripturis Sanctis non modo non peccasse, verum etiam juste vixisse referuntur cum hic viverent, congregare possemus, et interrogare, utrum essent sine peccato: quid fuisse responsuros putamus? Quantalibet fuerit in hoc corpore excellentia sanctitatis, si interrogari potuissent, una voce

Lamb without spot, who, by sacrifice of Himself once made, should take away the sins of the world, and sin, as Saint *John* saith, was not in Him. But all we the rest, although baptized, and born again in Christ, yet offend in many things; and if we say we have no sin, we deceive ourselves, and the truth is not in us.

EXPLANATION.—This Article, as far as the words "But all we the rest, although baptized," &c., is most sound. At this point, however, a gloss is required, not one of mine, but of the great St. Augustine (lib. "de Nat. et Grat. cont. Pelag.")—"When sins are treated of, for the honour of our Lord, I will have no mention whatever of the B. Virgin Mary; for we know that to her was given more grace, so as to conquer sin wholly, because she merited to conceive and bear Him, Who all agree was without sin. This Virgin then being excepted, if we could collect together all those saints, who in the Sacred Scriptures are said not only not to have sinned, but also to have lived justly, and were to ask them whether they were sinless, what do we think that they would answer? However great might have been the excellence of their sanctity in the

clamassent illud, quod ait Joannes Apostolus: Si dixerimus quia peccatum non habemus, ipsi nos seducimus, et veritas in nobis non est."

Ad hunc sensum explicandum censeo Articulum, et verba ipsa omnino favere: non enim dicit, *Omnes reliqui baptizati,* ubi ob universalitatem illius termini, includi videretur etiam B. Virgo, sed castius dicit: *nos reliqui,* ubi sine dubio non interponit B. Virginem inter communes fæces peccatorum, *propter honorem Domini,* præsertim dum eam Angelus ex Dei mandato, *gratiæ plenam et in mulieribus benedictam* pronunciavit. Si ergo illam includi voluissent Articuli conditores, aliquas saltem exceptiones honorarias addidissent, quod dum non fecerint, nec speciatim nominarint, putem illos cum Augustino, *Cum de peccatis agitur de S. Virgine Maria,* nullam prorsus habere velle quæstionem; immo per illum terminum restrictivum *(nos reliqui)* ipsam plane exclusisse charitative sentio. Et eo magis, quia subditur, *Nos reliqui* BAPTIZATI, de B. Virgine enim sub dubio semper fuit, an fuerit baptizata; forte enim ipsa fuit excepta flesh, if they could be asked the question, they would with one voice cry out that which the Apostle John says, 'If we say that we have no sin, we deceive ourselves, and the truth is not in us.'"

I think that the Article must be explained in this sense, and that the words are altogether favourable to the interpretation, for it is not said, "All we the rest:" where from the universal nature of the proposition, even the B. Virgin might seem to be included, but it is more properly "We the rest," in which expression, without doubt, the B. Virgin is not included with the common dregs of sin, "for the honour of our Lord," especially since the Angel by the command of God pronounced her "full of grace," and "blessed among women." If, therefore, the writers of the Articles had intended her to be included, they would at least have made some exceptions in her honour; and, since they did not do this, nor specially name her, I think that they, with St. Augustine, "when sins are treated of, will have no mention whatever of the B. Virgin Mary;" and further, by that restrictive expression ("we the rest"), I think that they plainly ex-

ab illa lege; nec mirum, quia ut pie Doctor 4. d. 4. q. 6 de ea fuisset ratio dispensandi : quia fortè habuit in conceptione Filii sui illam plenitudinem gratiæ, ad quam Deus disposuit eam pervenire. Illi igitur termini indefiniti in Articulo, non possunt rationabiliter extendi ad casum tam specialem et dubium.

cluded her. And I incline the more to this opinion, because there follows "We the rest, though BAPTIZED;" for there always was a doubt whether the B. Virgin ever was baptized, and perhaps she was excepted from that law. Nor need this be a cause for wonder; for, as the Doctor piously observes (4, d. 4, q. 6), there would have been a reason for dispensing in her case, because, perhaps, in the conception of her Son, she received that fulness of grace, to which God ordained that she should attain. I conclude, then, that those indefinite terms in the Article cannot reasonably be extended to a case so special and full of doubt.*

---

* [It may not be out of place to put on record what has been said by two English Roman Catholics, Mr. E. S. Ffoulkes and the Bishop of Birmingham, with regard to the dogma of the Immaculate Conception of the Blessed Virgin (which some persons, as they comprehend the doctrine, conceive to stand in direct opposition to certain propositions in this Article). Mr. Ffoulkes, who treats the subject most lucidly in his remarkable book, *Christendom's Divisions* (Longmans, 1865), thus writes, pp. 104-105 :—" All that is really implied by it [*i.e.*, the Immaculate Conception] is, that the Holy Ghost operated in the Blessed Virgin, from the first moment of her Conception, and throughout her life, that which He has, ever since the Day of Pentecost, operated in every man, woman, and child at the moment of their reception of Christian Baptism. He took away from the act of her Conception all that He takes away from each one of us at the instant of our Baptism; and that grace which, unfortunately, we are too apt to commence declining from the next moment afterwards, He by extraordinary privilege preserved ever afterwards intact through life in her alone, for whom alone was preserved the extraordinary honour of becoming His Spouse, and Mother of the Incarnate Word. For those who believe thoroughly in the Divine gift bestowed in Baptism, there can be no difficulty in believing in the Immaculate Conception of the Mother of God. It was but the anticipation of what is ac-

ARTICULUS XVI.—*De peccato post Baptismum.*

NON omne peccatum mortale post Baptismum voluntarie perpetratum est peccatum in Spiritum Sanctum, et irremissibile: proinde lapsis

ARTICLE XVI.—*Of Sin after Baptism.*

NOT every deadly sin willingly committed after Baptism is sin against the Holy Ghost, and unpardonable. Wherefore the grant of

complished in our own persons by the same Divine Agent, only carried out and perpetuated to perfection in her case. There is one instance recorded of a grade which is intermediate between her case and our own, upon indisputable testimony. It is that of S. John the Baptist: 'He shall be filled with the Holy Ghost,' said the angel Gabriel, 'even from his mother's womb.' Even this distinction has not been lost on the Church. Of all saints, S. John Baptist stands alone as commemorated on the day of his birth, as the Mother of God on the day of her Conception—both as without sin. I will add, before I quit the subject, that there is no fact more certain, or more unique, in the annals of Church history, than that, amidst the countless discoveries which have been reported of relics of saints in every age, there never has been so much as a breath of any discovery of any of that sacred body in which, and out of which, the Word was made Flesh. The Assumption of S. Mary would, at least, be one intelligible explanation of that extraordinary fact; it would be likewise but the natural consequence of her Immaculate Conception." Bishop **Ullathorne** likewise sets forth several important theological bearings of this doctrine with much clearness in the following passage:—" The confusion of two facts, which in their nature as in their causes are distinct and most completely apart, has given occasion to all the difficul-

ties which have attended as well the comprehension as the contemplation of the most pure and sublime mystery, which is under our consideration. A child derives not all its creation at one instant and from one source. For each child has two conceptions, and it is not of that one, which the word 'conception' commonly suggests, that we are now speaking. The body is transmitted through the parents, the soul is infused by God. The transmission of the body, whereby we are of the one body of Adam, is called by divines the *active* conception; the infusion of the soul, whereby the body receives its animation, is called the *passive* conception. The distinction between these two conceptions was not scientifically drawn at the period anterior to St. Thomas and St. Bonaventura. And the want of the distinction at an earlier period explains the seeming contradiction, for it is only an apparent one, which is found in some few of the Western fathers and other writers at an earlier period than the thirteenth century. Science has not been able to fix the period of animation; but, at whatever time it may take place, it is certain that the body is transmitted and organised ere the soul is infused, though the interval were but the least of which cognizance can be taken. For the infusion of the soul from God is consequent on the transmission of the body, and cannot be identical with that act or with its causes.

" We

a Baptismo in peccata, locus pœnitentiæ non est negandus. Post acceptum Spiritum Sanctum possumus a gratia data recedere, atque peccare, denuoque per gratiam Dei resurgere, ac resipiscere: ideoque illi damnandi sunt, qui se, quamdiu hic vivant, amplius non posse peccare affirmant, aut vere resipiscentibus veniæ locum denegant.

repentance is not to be denied to such as fall into sin after Baptism. After we have received the Holy Ghost, we may depart from grace given, and fall into sin, and by the grace of God we may arise again, and amend our lives. And therefore they are to be condemned, which say, they can no more sin as long as they live here, or deny the place of forgiveness to such as truly repent.

PARAPHRASIS.—Totus Articulus optimam continet doctrinam: illustratur tamen Prob. 27, et præcipuè Probl. 30.

EXPLANATION.—The whole Article contains excellent doctrine: it is, however, illustrated in Problem 27, and especially in Problem 30.

"We must further observe, as very important for understanding the subject, that the body before it has received the animating soul is not the subject, but only the cause of sin. Deriving from its origin the poison of concupiscence, it has its disordered energies awakened into activity by animation; and the soul, created and infused without grace, to which as a child of Adam it has lost all claim, becomes overwhelmed in its disorder, subjected to its blind confusion, and distorted from rectitude, until by the grace of Christ it is regenerated through baptism. But whilst through that holy sacrament the soul is raised up from injustice to life, the body remains subject to its infirmity, and has to be subdued and kept under, until it yields up the soul in death, for the flesh is only regenerated at the resurrection.

"Speaking with the strictest degree of accuracy, the transmission of flesh from Adam is not the conception of the Blessed Virgin Mary, but the conception of St. Ann. Of several mothers, the Scripture says, *she conceived a son*. But previous to animation, that flesh is not a human subject, and possesses no moral qualities. In fact, it is not Mary. Mary is truly conceived when her soul is created and infused into that body.

"Separating, then, these two periods of time, whatever may be the distance between them, the question regards not the embryo, which is not humanity, which has no personality, and which is incapable of spiritual grace: the question regards the moment of rational animation; of the reception, or, more truly, of the conception of the soul; and the instant of its union with the body."—*Bishop Ullathorne on the Immaculate Conception*, pp. 58-60. London: 1855.]

EXPLANATION FROM PROBLEM XXX.—The Anglican Confession manifestly agrees in Article XVI. with this universally received truth [that man may fall away after justification]. In Article IX. it was laid down that the regenerate could sin, as also in Article XV.; but they do not so fully declare the whole matter, because they can be explained to speak of a falling away which is not final, which alone is at this time controverted, but this Article solves the whole difficulty.

It is said then plainly—"After we have received the Holy Ghost;" which words, undoubtedly, imply a real, not a fictitious or seeming regeneration; else all the passages in the Acts of the Apostles, and elsewhere frequently in the Gospels, concerning the reception of the Holy Ghost, might be explained away, by saying that they ought to be understood, not of the real, but of a seeming regeneration; and consequently the whole truth of Holy Writ would be weakened. This, therefore, is not the true interpretation.

After that it is said in this Article, "May depart from grace given," (which, however, is in no wise true; for grace cannot be departed from), "and fall into sin"—namely, into sins which are properly opposed to grace, being mortal sins; for such alone by God's law deprive man of grace received.

But lest we should think that departure from grace, or committal of mortal sin, should be restricted to falling away for a time, it is opportunely added, "By the grace of God we may arise again;" it is not said that by grace we shall certainly rise again; which, however, ought to have been added, if it were meant to speak of final perseverance as a matter of certainty; but "we may arise"—that is, it is open to us by the grace of God to rise again, if we will; but, if we will not, we can also die in our sins. Nor were the words, "by the grace of God," added without forethought; because it is certain that, by the unaided powers of nature or of free will, we cannot rise again. The regenerate man then, after falling into sin, cannot of himself rise again; nor is the grace of God due to him: for then, according to the Apostle, it would be no more grace, as all the Doctors teach after him.

Whence, then, can there be any certainty of final perseverance?—seeing that there is no law for the infallible efficacious conjunction of grace and nature stained by mortal sin. This is the plainest meaning of this Article, which will appear even more clearly if we refer to the Book of Homilies,

where it is said, after much more on the fall of the regenerate, "They will be given over into the power of the devil, who exercises his power over all reprobates or forsaken of God, as Saul and Judas." They are compared to Saul and Judas, of whose final fall no one doubts; because each of them, being finally impenitent, and dying in the act of mortal sin, in fact was the destroyer of himself.

Articulus XVII.—De Prædestinatione et Electione.

PRÆDESTINATIO ad vitam, est æternum Dei propositum, quo, ante jacta mundi fundamenta, suo consilio, nobis quidem occulto, constanter decrevit, eos, quos in Christo elegit ex hominum genere, a maledicto et exitio liberare, atque (ut vasa in honorem efficta) per Christum, ad æternam salutem adducere. Unde qui tam præclaro Dei beneficio sunt donati, illi Spiritu Ejus, opportuno tempore operante, secundum propositum Ejus, vocantur; vocationi per gratiam parent; justificantur gratis; adoptantur in filios [Dei]*, unigeniti Ejus Filii Jesu Christi imagini efficiuntur conformes; in bonis operibus sancte ambulant; et demum ex Dei misericordia pertingunt ad sempiternam felicitatem.

Quemamodum prædestinationis et electionis nostræ in Christo pia con-

Article XVII.—Of Predestination and Election.

PREDESTINATION to Life is the everlasting purpose of God, whereby (before the foundations of the world were laid) he hath constantly decreed by his counsel secret to us, to deliver from curse and damnation those whom he hath chosen in Christ out of mankind, and to bring them by Christ to everlasting salvation, as vessels made to honour. Wherefore, they which be endued with so excellent a benefit of God be called according to God's purpose, by his Spirit working in due season: they through Grace obey the calling: they be justified freely; they be made sons of God by adoption: they be made like the image of his only-begotten Son Jesus Christ: they walk religiously in good works, and at length, by God's mercy, they attain to everlasting felicity.

As the godly consideration of Predestination and our Election in

---

* [The word "Dei" does not occur in some versions of the Latin Articles.]

sideratio, dulcis, suavis, et ineffabilis consolationis plena est, vere piis, et iis qui sentiunt in se vim Spiritus Christi, facta carnis, et membra, quæ adhuc sunt semper terram, mortificantem animumque ad cœlestia et superna rapientem; tum quia fidem nostram de æterna salute consequenda per Christum plurimum stabilit atque confirmat, tum quia amorem nostrum in Deum vehementer accendit, ita hominibus curiosis, carnalibus, et Spiritu Christi destitutis, ob oculos perpetuo versari prædestinationis Dei sententiam periculosissimum est præcipitium, unde illos Diabolus protrudit impurissimæ vitæ securitatem.

Christ, is full of sweet, pleasant, and unspeakable comfort to godly persons, and such as feel in themselves the working of the Spirit of Christ, mortifying the works of the flesh, and their earthly members, and drawing up their mind to high and heavenly things, as well because it doth greatly establish and confirm their faith of eternal Salvation to be enjoyed through Christ, as because it doth fervently kindle their love towards God: So, for curious and carnal persons, lacking the Spirit of Christ, to have continually before their eyes the sentence of God's Predestination is a most dangerous downfall, whereby the Devil doth thrust them either into desperation, or into wretchlessness of most unclean living, no less perilous than desperation.

Deinde, promissiones divinas sic amplecti oportet, ut nobis in Sacris Literis generaliter propositæ sunt; et Dei voluntas in nostris actionibus ea sequenda est, quam in verbo Dei habemus diserte revelatam.

Furthermore, we must receive God's promises in such wise, as they be generally set forth to us in holy Scripture: and, in our doings, that Will of God is to be followed, which we have expressly declared unto us in the Word of God.

PARAPHRASIS.—Catholicus est, et fuse declaratur Problemate 1.

EXPLANATION.—This Article is Catholic, and is explained fully in Problem 1.

EXPLANATION FROM PROBLEM I.—"The Predestination of the Saints is nothing else than the foreknowledge and preparation of the benefits bestowed by God, by which most certainly all who are freed are freed."

(*St. Aug. l. "de bon. Persev."* c. 14).—" Predestination is the fore-ordaining of anyone to glory in the first place, and to other things in order to glory." (*Scot.* 3. *d.* 7. *qu.* 7.) "Predestination is the order of election by the Divine Will, whereby beings endowed with understanding are elected to grace and glory." (Common definition.) With these three definitions agrees the description of Predestination in Article XVII. Unless I mistake, it rightly and exactly explains the question, for what follows, "those chosen in Christ out of mankind," is no more than St. Paul says, "Having predestinated us by Jesus Christ to himself" (Eph. i. 5)—that is, for his honour. The meaning, therefore, is that Christ is the first of all the predestinate, both in excellency of dignity, because predestinated to the highest supernatural gifts, and in excellency of end, because that for His glory all others were predestinated.

ARTICULUS XVIII.—*De speranda æterna salute tantum in Nomine Christi.*

SUNT et illi anathematizandi, qui dicere audent unumquemque in lege aut secta quam profitetur esse servandum, modo juxta illam et lumen naturæ accurate vixerit; cum Sacræ Literæ tantum Jesu Christi Nomen prædicent, in quo salvos fieri homines oporteat.

ARTICLE XVIII. — *Of obtaining eternal salvation only by the Name of Christ.*

THEY also are to be had accursed that presume to say, that every man shall be saved by the law or sect which he professeth, so that he be diligent to frame his life according to that law and the light of nature. For Holy Scripture doth set out unto us only the Name of Jesus Christ, whereby men must be saved.*

---

* ["This Article," remarks Dr. Neale, "anathematizes those who say that every man shall be saved by the law or sect that he professeth, so that he be diligent to frame his life according to that law and to the light of nature. The English Church, then, requires us to receive, as of faith, the diametrically opposite opinion, and to hold that 'no man shall be saved by the law or sect that he professeth, so he acts up to the light of nature.' That is, that if he be saved, it will not be on account of his having belonged to it, nor on account of his having acted up to the light of nature. But we are not required to believe in the necessary damnation of heathens and heretics—that not being the proposition rigorously opposite to that condemned."—"Open Questions:" *Neale's Lectures on Church Difficulties.* London: Cleaver, 1852.]

PARAPHRASIS.—Catholicus est.

EXPLANATION.—This Article is Catholic.

ARTICULUS XIX.—*De Ecclesia.*

ECCLESIA Christi visibilis est cœtus fidelium, in quo verbum Dei purum prædicatur, et Sacramenta, quoad ea quæ necessario exigantur, juxta Christi institutum, recte administrantur. Sicut erravit Ecclesia Hierosolymitana, Alexandrina, et Antiochena; ita et erravit Ecclesia Romana, non solum quoad agenda, et cæremoniarum ritus, verum in his etiam quæ credenda sunt.

ARTICLE XIX.—*Of the Church.*

THE visible Church of Christ is a congregation of faithful men, in the which the pure Word of God is preached, and the Sacraments be duly ministered according to Christ's ordinance in all those things that of necessity are requisite to the same. As the Church of Jerusalem, Alexandria, and Antioch have erred, so also the Church of Rome hath erred, not only in their living and manner of ceremonies, but also in matters of Faith.*

PARAPHRASIS. — Prior Paragraphus sanus est, nullum enim exclusivum habet, prorsus tamen inadæquatus est, sicut homo est animal bipes, est propositio vera, licet non adæquata. Posterior glossandus, ubi etiam dicit Ecclesiam Romanam errasse in rebus fidei : advertendum est ibi contradistingui Ecclesiam Romanam a cæteris particularibus

EXPLANATION.—The first paragraph of this Article is sound, having in it nothing to exclude the truth. It is, however, inadequate as a definition, as it would be to say, "Man is an animal having two feet." The statement is quite true, though inadequate. The latter part requires explanation. Where, then, it says that the Church of Rome hath erred

---

* [This paragraph may be taken to mean no more than that local churches, national communions, or even whole patriarchates—if acting independently of the other parts of the Christian Family—cannot look to be miraculously preserved from error " in matters of faith." This is rendered clearer from the statement in Art. XX., that " the Church (*i.e.*, the Universal Church, not the Church of England, or any particular church) ... hath authority in controversies of Faith."]

Ecclesiis, quia pariformiter de Hierosolymitana, Alexandrina, in quo sensu si dixeris errasse de facto, non est contra fidem, licet contra veritatem : Ecclesiam autem Romanam sic aliquando contradistingui, antiquitas testatur. Hieronymus enim epist. 85, Episcopum Romæ pari gradu condistinguit Episcopo Eugubii, id est, prout præcisè Episcopus urbis; secus si etiam ut Episcopus orbis. Innocent. IV. c. *Apostolicæ de re indicata*, omnino distinguit Ecclesiam Romanam ab Ecclesia universali etiam representativa, sic Trid. sess. 14. frequens est etiam apud Doctores præsertim apud Bellar. de summo Pontif. l. 4. c. 4. et Mirandulam de fide et ordine credendi, Theoremate 6, §. Quapropter etiam advertendum, Ecclesia vero Romana, frequentius aliter sumitur, sicut in Concilio Constant. sess. 8. per Romanam Ecclesiam, Ecclesiam Universalem intelligi vult; et eam errasse non asserit Articulus, quod **solum** est de fide.

in matters of faith, we must notice that the Church of Rome is spoken of as distinct from other particular churches ; for the same language is used concerning the churches of Jerusalem and Alexandria ; in which sense, if a man say that she has indeed erred, the statement is not contrary to the *faith*, though it be contrary to the *truth*. At the same time, antiquity testifies that the Roman Church is thus sometimes distinguished from others ; for St. Jerome (*in Ep.* 85) speaks of the Bishop of Rome as in the same rank with the Bishop of Eugubium, so far, that is, as he is simply bishop of the city ; but the case is different when he is considered as bishop of the world. Innocent IV. (c. "*Apostolicæ de re Judicata*) wholly distinguishes the Roman Church from the Universal Church even representatively; and so, too, the Council of Trent (Sess. 14); and this is also a common opinion with the doctors: especially see Bellarmine "*De Summo Pont.*" (l. 4, c. 4) : and Mirandula "*De Fide et Ordine Credendi (Theor.* 6, § *Quapropter etiam advertendum*). But the Roman Church is very often spoken of otherwise, as in the Coun-

cil of Constance (Sess. 8), by the Roman Church is meant the Church Universal, and the Article does not assert her to have erred, which alone is of the faith.

Articulus XX.—*De Ecclesiæ authoritate.*

Ecclesia potestatem habet decernendi ritus et ceremonias et dirimendi controversias in fide.* Ecclesiæ non licet quicquam instituere, quod verbo Dei adversetur, nec unum Scripturæ locum sic exponere potest, ut alteri contradicat. Quare licet Ecclesia sit divinorum testis et conservatrix, attamen ut adversus eos nihil decernere, ita præter illos nihil credendum de necessitate salutis debet obtrudere.

Article XX.—*Of the authority of the Church.*

THE Church hath power to decree Rites and Ceremonies, and authority in controversies of Faith; and yet it is not lawful for the Church to ordain anything that is contrary to God's Word written; neither may it so expound one place of Scripture that it be repugnant to another. Wherefore, although the Church be a witness and a keeper of Holy Writ, yet as it ought not to decree anything against the same, so besides the same ought it not to enforce anything to be believed for necessity of salvation.

Paraphrasis.—Priora verba clara sunt, et omni antiquitati consona, unde Aug. l. de Utilitate Credendi, contra Manichæos, culmen authori-

Explanation.—The commencement is clear, and in agreement with all antiquity, as Augustine (*lib.* "*de Utilit. Cred.*"), against the Manichees,

---

* [The first paragraph of this Article—neither in the Latin MS. signed by Convocation in 1562, nor in the English MS. signed in 1571, nor in either of the editions published by Bishop Jewel—runs as follows in some versions (*e.g.*, Wolfe's, 1563):—

"Habet ecclesia ritus (sive cæremonias) statuendi jus, et in fidei controversiis authoritatem; quamvis," etc. After the word "Dei" *scripto* is inserted; and after "divinorum" the word *librorum*.—Vide Editor's Preface.]

tatis quoad prædicta in Ecclesia consistere declarat.

Verba subsequentia non minus clara : scriptura enim secundum omnes veteres est regula certa veritatis, unde Aug. l. de baptismo c. 3 :— *Quis nesciat Sanctam Scripturam Canonicam, tam Veteris quam Novi Testamenti, omnibus posteriorum Episcoporum literis ita præponi, ut de illa omnino dubitari et disceptari non possit, utrum verum vel utrum rectum sit, quicquid in ea Scriptura constiterit, etc.*

Quod autem subditur in Articulo, Ecclesiam esse testem et conservatricem sacræ Scripturæ valde conforme est D. Paulo, qui eam vocat *firmamentum veritatis*, et Joanni in Apocalypsi qui eam vocat, *Civitatem habentem fundamenta duodecim, et in ipsis duodecim nomina duodecim Apostolorum:* scilicet qui eam prædicationibus et sacris scriptis suis fundaverunt. Valde etiam confirmatur Articulus ex sententia Augustini contra Epistolam fundamenti : *Evangelio non crederem, nisi me Ecclesiæ Catholicæ commoveret authoritas.* Unde ipsa semper declaravit veras à pseudo-scripturis, ut patet Carth. 6. can. 46. et in posterioribus, de quo supra ;

declares the chief authority in all such matters is with the Church.

The following part is no less clear ; for, according to all the ancients, Scripture is the sure rule of truth, whence St. Augustine (*lib.* "*de Baptismo,*" c. 3) says, "Who is ignorant that all Sacred Canonical Scripture, whether of the Old or New Testament, is so to be preferred to all writings of subsequent Bishops, that there never may be doubt or dispute whether anything established by that Scripture be true and right."

And what comes next in the Article, that the Church is the witness and keeper of Holy Writ, is quite in agreement with St. Paul, who calls her the "ground of the truth ;" and St. John in the Apocalypse calls her "The city having twelve foundations, and in them the names of the twelve Apostles of the Lamb" (Rev. xxi. 14),—that is, that they founded her by their preaching and holy writings. The Article, too, is strongly confirmed by the saying of St. Augustine—"I would not believe the Gospel, unless the authority of the Catholic Church induced me." So that she has always distinguished between true and false Scripture, as is

quam veritatem optime declarat Molina i. p. disp. i. art. 2.

Postrema verba Articuli glossam interlinearem deposcunt: ubi enim dicitur, *Ita præter illos nihil credendum de necessitate salutis debet obtrudere.* Istud *præter* intelligi debet, quod nec actu nec δυνάμει in eis continetur, hoc est, quod nec in terminis nec ut consequentiæ inde deducitur, seu quod *inde probari non potest,* ut astruitur Articulo sexto. Quod sanum ferre sensum æstimo, nempe illum Augustini contra Cresc. i. c. 33. *Quamvis hujus rei certe de Scripturis Canonicis non proferatur exemplum, earundem tamen etiam in hac re a nobis teneretur veritas, cum hoc facimus quod universæ placet* Ecclesiæ, *quam* ipsarum *scripturarum commendat authoritas ut quia S. Scriptura fallere non potest,* quisquis *falli metuit, eandem Ecclesiam consulat, quam sine ulla ambiguitate S. Scriptura* demonstrat.

Adde etiam, scripturas divinas non de iis solum instruere quæ scripta sunt, sed de iis etiam quæ non sunt scripta, ut patet i. ad Cor. xi. 2. Ephes. ii. Hujusmodi ergo Ecclesia potest pro-

clear from the Council of Carthage (6 *Can.* 46); and, subsequently, which truth is most ably shown by Molina (1 *p. disp.* 1, *art.* 2).

The latter parts of the Article require interpretation line by line; where it is said, "Beside them ought nothing," &c. By *beside* must be understood what is not either actually or virtually in them—that is, neither expressed in terms nor can be deduced as a consequence from them; or which "may not be proved thereby," as is said in the sixth Article. And I think that these expressions have a sound meaning, according to St. Augustine (*Against Cresconius*, 1, c. 33).

Moreover, the Scriptures themselves sometimes refer to ordinances and traditions not contained in Scripture, as 1 Cor. xi. 2. Things of this kind, therefore, the Church has

ponere credenda, et ex Scripturis probari possunt; nec adversatur **Articulus.**

Quando etiam dixi, in terminis vel in hac consequentia; volo dicere, non solum ut consequentiæ fidei; sed etiam evidenti lumine naturæ, verbi gratia, in hac consequentia, Christus homo est, ergo habet cor, sanguinem, cerebrum, etc. Consequens enim illud est de fide, ut Doctores Theologi communiter asserunt, vel saltem est veritas theologica secundum omnes.

power to propose to our faith, and they can be proved by Scripture, nor is the Article against this.

Again: when I said above, "either expressed in terms or deduced as a consequence from them," I mean, not only as a consequence when viewed by the light of faith, but even by the light of nature; as, for instance, in the following consequences. Christ is a Man: therefore He has a heart, blood, brain, &c. For such consequences are of faith, as theologians commonly say; or at least they are theological truths, as all allow.

Articulus XXI.—*De Authoritate Conciliorum Generalium.*

GENERALIA Concilia sine jussu et voluntate Principum congregari non possunt: et ubi convenerunt, quia ex hominibus constant, qui non omnes spiritu et verbo Dei reguntur, et errare possunt, et interdum erra-

Article XXI.—*Of the Authority of General Councils.*[*]

GENERAL Councils may not be gathered together without the commandment and will of Princes. And when they be gathered together (forasmuch as they be an assembly of men, whereof all be not governed

---

[*] [In this Article it is to be carefully noted that no exception is taken against the **Western** Patriarch presiding over or confirming and promulgating the decision and decrees of General Councils — only against his exercising the **power to** call them together. Furthermore, it does not assert that General Councils can err in things pertaining to the Faith or necessary to salvation. "Things pertaining to God," is both a quaint expression and an expression of great latitude. Roman Catholics would not deny that they **might err in any** minor matters brought before them for consideration. The Council of Nicæa determined the controversy concerning the keeping of Easter—an important but not a fundamental or essential point. General Councils **have** often discussed other subjects than the Faith.]

runt, etiam in his quæ ad normam pietatis* pertinent ; ideoque quæ ab illis constituuntur ut ad salutem necessaria, neque robur habent neque authoritatem, nisi ostendi possint è sacris literis esse desumpta.

PARAPHRASIS.—Priora verba videntur confirmari authoritate Hieronymi Apol. 2, contra Rufinum, ubi ex hoc capite quoddam Concilium rejicit, dicens : *Quis Imperator hanc Synodum jussit congregari ?* Quasi velit, necessariam hac in parte jussionem Imperatoris, et sic observatum patet in omnibus fere Conciliis veteribus, ut de Nicæno ex jussione Constantini ; Sardicensi, Constantii et Constantis, Constantinop. I. Senioris Theodosii ; ut referunt Socrates et Nicephorus. Per se quidem loquendo, id est, spectando solum jus divinum, Concilia possunt cogi sine

with the Spirit and Word of God) they may err, and sometimes have erred, even in things pertaining unto God. Therefore, things ordained by them as necessary to salvation have neither strength nor authority, until it may be declared that they be taken out of Holy Scripture.†

EXPLANATION.—The commencement seems to be confirmed by the authority of St. Jerome (*Apol.* 2, *cont. Rufinum*), where he rejects a Council on this ground, saying, " What Emperor ordered this Synod to be convened ?" As though he meant that the command was necessary ; and the same remark is obvious in respect of almost all the ancient Councils, as the Nicene summoned by Constantine ; the Sardican, by Constantius and Constans ; the Constantinopolitan, by Theodosius the elder, as is related by Socrates and Nicephorus. But, speaking of

---

* [Some versions have " ad Deum " after " pietatis."]

† [St. Gregory Nazianzen well illustrates the consistency of this Article with a belief in the infallibility of Œcumenical Councils, by his own language on the subject on different occasions. In the following passage he anticipates the Article :—" My mind is, if I must write the truth, to keep clear of every conference of Bishops, for of conference never saw I good come, or a remedy so much as an increase of evils. For there is strife and ambition, and these have the upper hand of reason" (*Ep.* lv.). Yet, on the other hand, he speaks elsewhere of " the Holy Council in Nicæa, and that band of chosen men whom the Holy Ghost brought together" Orat. xxi. (*Tract* 90, p. 22, 2nd Edit.).]

interventu potestatis Principum, ut constat de Hierosolymitano; nec hoc potuit Hieronymus negare; per accidens tamen ob circumstantias temporum, et locorum, debet omnino consensus, immo et jussio Principum subinde præmitti. De consensu patet, ob bonum et pacem publicam. De jussione etiam æquè constat, quando verbi gratiâ Episcopi, vel quorum interest, adesse conciliis, nolint parere citationi Ecclesiasticæ (vel ob alias causas id genus multas) tunc enim Principes authoritate sibi à Deo commissa justè possunt adversus eos edicere; de hoc lege Durand. de mod. Concil. Gener. celeb. rubr. 71. Unde Martianus ad Leonem, *Si*, inquit, *onerosum est, ut tu ad has partes venias, hoc ipsum nobis propriis litteris tua sanctitas manifestet, quatenus in omnem Orientem et in omnem Thraciam et Illyricum sacræ nostræ literæ dirigantur, ut ad aliquem definitum locum qui nobis placuerit omnes Episcopi conveniant.* Sic etiam Gregorius, Theodoricum Francorum Regem, Epist. 54. l. 9. Registri, hortatur, ut contra Simoniacos qui per Regnum suum impunè grassabantur, Synodum *jubeat* congregari, sic etiam V Synodus

Councils in themselves—that is, considering only the Divine law—they can be convened without the intervention of the power of Princes, as was the case in the Council of Jerusalem; nor could St. Jerome deny this. Accidentally, however, owing to circumstances of times and places, the consent and even the commandment of Princes ought to precede Councils. As far as their consent goes, this is evident for the sake of public good and peace; nor is there any more difficulty as regards their commandment, when, for instance, Bishops or others, who ought to be present in Councils, refuse to obey the ecclesiastical citation (or for many other causes of that sort); for then Princes, by the authority entrusted to them by God, may justly issue edicts against them. On this point, consult Durandus ("*de Mod. Concil. Gen. celeb. rubr.* 71"). So that Martian wrote to Leo, "If it be irksome for you to come to these parts, let your holiness show this to us by your letters, how far our sacred letters may be directed to all the East, and all Thrace and Illyricum, that all the Bishops should come together to one prescribed place, which

quæ est secunda Constant. actione 2. habet. *Hic proximis diebus præcedente pio jussu Christo amantissimi ac Deo custoditi Imperatoris, nobis convenit præsens nunc sancta Synodus;* et sic sanctitatum testantur concilia allater, nec aliud in hujus Articuli infertur.

Verba sequentia æquè facilis sunt concoctionis, magnam enim latitudinem habet illa clausula (*etiam in rebus ad Deum spectantibus*) Concilia enim Generalia errare posse in rebus, quæ fidem aut mores ad salutem necessarios non concernunt, communis est Doctorum, ut patet in decreto Innoc. et Panormitanus ibi, sic etiam D. Tho. in Quodlibet, et optime declarat Cano in locis l. 5. c. 5. qu. 4. Bellarm. etiam de Rom. Pontif. lib. 2. c. 16. §. ubi observandum est, maneat ergo clausula illa

shall be determined by us. So, too, St. Gregory exhorts Theodoric, King of the Franks (*Ep.* 54, l. 9), that he would *order* a synod to meet against the simoniacal offenders who infested his kingdom with impunity. And so, too, the Fifth Synod, which is the second of Constantinople (*act* 2), has as follows:—" Here, within these last few days, the pious command of our most Christ-loving and divinely-guarded Emperor preceding, the present holy synod gathered together to us." And that this was repeatedly done, the acts of other Councils show, nor can anything more be inferred from the tenor of this Article.

The subsequent words are no less easy to be explained, for that clause ("even in things pertaining unto God") has great latitude. For that General Councils may err in matters which do not concern the faith or morals, in things necessary to salvation, is the common opinion of the Doctors, as is plain from the decree of Innocent and Panormitanus; as well as St. Thomas in "Quodlibet," and as is excellently set forth by Canus in the "*Loci Theologici*" (l. 5, c. 5, qu. 4); and by Bellarmine, "*de*

(*etiam in rebus ad Deum spectantibus*) modo non sint necessaria respectu fidei et bonorum morum; quod nec ibi asseritur.

Ultima verba sententiam veterum, et omnium fere modernorum declarant: non enim possunt de non hæretica, facere propositionem hæreticum, ut in causis fidei; nec cudere Artic. Fidei, ut rectè Suarez de Trip. Virt. Disp. 2. § 6. n. 10. Sed solum ex abditioribus Scripturæ locis, et Apost. dictis, veritatem cruere, I. ut *intelligatur illustrius, quod antea credebatur obscurius;* ut loquitur Lerinensis c. 17. Cano etiam in locis l. 12. fol. 353. ex D. Th. dicit, fidem nostram non inniti revelationibus aliis præter eas, quas Apostoli et Prophetæ, authores videlicet canonicorum Librorum, ediderunt. Et confirmat ex D. Paulo. unde Doct. Subt. 4. d. xi. qu. 3. agens de definitione Concilii Lateranensis, dicit non fuisse in potestate Ecclesiæ facere istud verum aut non verum (scilicet transubstantiationem) sed Dei instituentis. Ecclesiæ quidem est (*directa in hoc ut creditur à Spiritu veritatis*) Rom. Pont. (lib. 2, c. 16, § *Ubi observandum*). The clause ("even in things pertaining to God") may, therefore, stand, provided only they be not matters necessary in respect of faith and morals, which is not asserted in the Article.

The last paragraph expresses the opinions of the ancient and of almost all modern authors; for they cannot make a proposition heretical which is not heretical, as is rightly stated by Gerson in the question "*An liceat appellare in causis fidei;*" nor can they concoct Articles of Faith, as says Suarez rightly, "*de Trip. Virt.*" (disp. 2, § 6, n. 10). All that they can do is to extract the truth from the more abstruse parts of Holy Scripture, and the sayings of the Apostles, in order that "that may be more clearly understood which before was more obscurely believed;" as says Vincent of Lerins (c. 17). Melchior Canus, too, "*Loci Theol.*" (l. 12, fol. 353), says, from St. Thomas, that our faith does not rest upon other revelations than those which the Apostles and Prophets—the authors, that is to say, of the Canonical books—have set forth; and he confirms this from St. Paul. Whence

intellectum à Deo traditum in Scripturis explicare, ut recte ipse. Et hoc facit Ecclesia, dum aliquam veritatem definire dicitur: non enim novis revelationibus innititur, sed antiquis, in Scripturis et dictis Apostolorum. Unde Doctor ibidem dicit, quod in symbolo illo sub Innocent. III. in Concil. Lat. c. Firmiter credimus, magis explicitè ponitur veritas aliquot credendorum, quam habebatur Symbolo Apostolorum, vel Athanasii, vel Nicæni; non ergo nova fides, sed vetusta magis explicatur, sic etiam Molina I. quæst. i. art. 2. disp. 1. dicit: Quod concursus quo Spiritus Sanctus præsto adest Ecclesiæ, non est constituendum aliquid esse de fide, quod antea non erat de fide; sed solum assistit ad declarandum ea quæ mediate, vel immediate spectant ad fide. Et sicut Ecclesiæ non est potestas facere, at solum declarare fidelibus, quid debeat certo teneri de fide; sic nec etiam est potestas facere sacram Scripturam, vel addere vel diminuere Canonicos libros. Sic etiam Turrecremata, et Vega supra Trident. l. I. c. 6. Valentia 2. 2. d. 1. quæst. I. et alii, et D. Thom. 2.

the Subtle Doctor[*] (4, d. 11, qu. 3), treating of the definition of the Lateran Council, says that to make that point true or not true (he is speaking of *transubstantiation*) was not in the power of the Church, but of God, who instituted the Sacrament. It is, indeed, the office of the Church (directed in this as is believed by the Spirit of Truth) to explain the mind of God as set forth in the Scriptures, as he says rightly; and the Church does this, when she is said to define any truth; for she does not trust to new revelations, but to the old ones, hidden in the Scriptures and in the words of the Apostles, as is the constant opinion of the Doctors. Whence Scotus says in the same place, that in the Creed set forth by Innocent III. in the Lateran Council (c. *Firmiter Credimus*), the truth of certain matters of faith is asserted more explicitly than it was in the Apostles' Creed, or the Athanasian or the Nicene; but there was not for that reason any new faith, but the old faith more fully explained. And so, too, Molina (1 qu. 1, art. 2, disp. 1) says, "that the presence of the Holy

---

[* *i.e.* Johannes Duns Scotus.]

2. q. 1. art. 7. expressè docet: *Articulos fidei post tempora Apostolorum non crevisse;* quod non alium potest habere sensum, quam illum quem posuimus, crevissent enim, si Ecclesia sua definitione efficeret, ut aliqui Articuli jam essent de fide, qui antea non erant, ut recte Conink De Actibus Supernaturalibus, disp. 12. dub. 6. Et ex hoc convincitur. Nam secundum Apostolum, Ephes. 2. superædificamur *supra fundamentum Apostolorum et Prophetarum;* non igitur aliud fundamentum, nec alia fides, quam ipsorum. Huic conforme est illud Cyp. ep. 74. *Si in aliquo nataverit et vacillaverit veritas, ad originem Dominicam, Evangelicam,* et Apostolicam additionem revertamur, et inde surgat actus *nostri ratio, unde et ordo et origo surrexit.*

Ghost with the Church is not for the purpose of making anything of faith which was not before of faith, but only for the purpose of declaring those things which directly or indirectly affect the faith; and as in the Church there is no power to make anything of faith which was not so before, but only to declare to the faithful what ought for certain to be held as of faith, so neither is there any power to make Holy Scripture, nor to add to or diminish from the Canonical Books." So, too, say Turrecremata and Vega on the Council of Trent (l. 1, c. 6), Valentia (2, 2, d. 1, qu. 1), and others besides St. Thomas, who expressly teaches (2, 2, qu. 1, art. 7), "that the Articles of Faith have not increased since the times of the Apostles," which can have no other meaning than the one which we have laid down; since they would have increased, had the Church by her definitions made any Articles to be of faith now which were not so before, as is rightly said by Conink, "*De Actibus Supernat.*" (disp. 12, dub. 6). And it is proved as follows, according to the Apostle (Eph. ii. 20), we "are built upon the foundation of the Apostles and Prophets."

There is, therefore, no other foundation, nor any other faith, than theirs. With this agrees that passage of St. Cyprian (*Ep.* 74)—" If the truth have at all moved or been shaken, let us return to the fountain, to the tradition of our Lord, of the Gospel, and of the Apostles; and from thence let the method of our acts take its rise, whence the order and the beginning itself arose."

ARTICULUS XXII.—*De Purgatorio.*

DOCTRINA Romanensium de Purgatorio, de Indulgentiis, de Veneratione et Adoratione tum Imaginum, tum Reliquiarum; necnon de Invocatione Sanctorum, res est futilis, inaniter conficta, et nullis Scripturarum testimoniis innititur, immo verbo Dei contradicit.

PARAPHRASIS.—Examinatus est Probl. 37.

ARTICLE XXII.—*Of Purgatory.*

THE Romish Doctrine concerning Purgatory, Pardons, Worshipping and Adoration, as well of Images as of Reliques, and also Invocation of Saints, is a fond thing vainly invented, and grounded upon no warranty of Scripture, but rather repugnant to the Word of God.

EXPLANATION.—This Article is examined in Problem 37.

EXPLANATION FROM PROBLEM XXXVII.—These words are, without doubt, at first sight most difficult. But it must be observed that, by the terms of this Article, it is not the Invocation of Saints absolutely, or in itself, that is condemned, but *the Romish doctrine.* If we would, therefore, see the meaning of this decision or censure of theirs, we must examine the Roman doctrine; not, however, what the Romans or Catholics (for the words are synonymous in their mode of speaking) hold, but what is supposed to be their doctrine. This, then, we must discover, not from the writings of Catholics, but from those of their opponents.

Dr. Andrewes in his Answer to c. 2 of Cardinal Peronnius (fol. 28),

like Calvin, supposes that our prayers are addressed to the Saints ultimately and absolutely, and offered, as it were, to so many deities, as he endeavours to show at length—not indeed from the agreement of the Doctors, but from the wording of some of the hymns. This, then, is the doctrine which is condemned in the Article as vain; which we, too, abjure as impious. What cause is there, then, for wonder if the people, when imbued with such calumnies, are opposed to sound and Catholic doctrine?

The controversy, then, is not about words, but about the *meaning* of words, as Bellarmine rightly remarks. Dr. Andrewes knew quite well that all the Catholic doctors, without exception, when speaking doctrinally, have always condemned that mode of addressing the Saints; and the Church herself declared the same at Trent. So, why should we refer to the hymns? The sum of the matter is, that the Anglican Confession has decided nothing against the faith; but has condemned an impious heathen notion, falsely imputed to the Church.

In exactly the same manner, and in words of the same purport in the same Article, they reject, not purgatory, indulgences, the worshipping of relics and images in itself, but as before the *Romish doctrine* on all these points—that is, a doctrine falsely imputed to us. Purgatory, they think, is a place invented by us, making the Cross of Christ of none effect, &c. They have many wonderful ideas of this kind. On the subject of indulgences, they think that they are a kind of merchandize of the Pope's; as though he, at his own will, freed the living or dead from all punishment due to their sins (I am speaking throughout of the Calvinists). On the worship of images and relics, they think that we pay them the worship properly called *latria*, and having them for its object, and so make idols of them, like the heathen. These wicked calumnies and fables of wicked men, under the name of *Romish doctrine*, they reject as absurd; we detest them as supremely injurious to the Spouse of God.

Very many of them admit purgatory in itself, so far, that is, as the substance of the Church's definition, especially in the Council of Florence, namely, *a place of purifying and cleansing*, as St. Cyprian says (tom. i. ep. 52), though the manner of purifying and cleansing is not very clearly defined. Indulgences, too, as they are defined by the Council of Trent— that is, a certain judicial absolution or relaxation, as in God's stead, of [temporal] penalties on account of sins (as the Schoolmen say) with St.

Cyprian (tom. 1, ep. 14), and Tertullian (tom. 2, l. ad Martyres, c. 1, and elsewhere), **they do not reject**; nor is this only what was due to the Church from the penitential discipline, as the Calvinists say; for, as St. Cyprian says in that place, "They who have received a writ from the martyrs, can be helped by their intercession before God," not therefore only before the Church. St. Cyprian asks the martyrs, however, "to weigh carefully the requests of those who ask, as the friends of the Lord, and those who will hereafter judge together with Him, both the state and the deeds and the merits of every one" (ep. 11 or 15). He gives them a method how to ask from the prelates of the Church the remission of the penalties, or the satisfaction due to God for the sinners. Indeed, Chemnitz himself, in controversy with Bellarmine, owns that Augustine, Cyprian, and Tertullian frequently recognise indulgences, in the sense spoken of, as well as the worship of images and relics, as laid down in the Councils of Nicæa, Florence, and Trent; and none of these points are denied in the Articles of the Anglican Confession. Indeed, the more learned of my countrymen, with whom I have often conversed, fully receive these matters; and in our conferences have ingenuously owned that they are all agreeable to primitive antiquity; but that there is a sacred spiritual treasury made up of the merits of Christ and the Saints, and had in acceptance with God, they do not think is equally clearly set forth in Scripture and the writings of the Fathers. On our side Mayron, with some few others, held the same opinion, and did not think such a belief necessary for establishing the truth of indulgences.

As respects the veneration of relics and the Cross of Christ, Dr. Andrewes (Respons. ad c. 18 Peronnii), Casaubon (in Exercit. Baronii ad annum, p. 34 et alibi), together with some others following. St. Cyril (in Catech. 4), St. Jerome (ad Marcellum), St. Augustine, and others, allow a certain worship, or *a certain reverential honour,* towards sacred images, in agreement with St. Chrysostom in his liturgy—that is, *a religious bowing to an image*—adds after the others Dr. Montagu (Respons. ad Heigham and Appello Cæsarem, c. 22), which reverence the Greeks have always paid, as is shown by Curopalata (De Officialibus).

Concerning Purgatory, the older writers among them allowed it, as is clear from Fox speaking of Latimer; nor did Latimer absolutely deny it. I am not, however, engaged in an inquiry into the opinions of individuals, having shown what is defined in the Anglican confession; where, as I said,

not the use of the Church, but an abuse calumniously imputed to her, is condemned. On this point we shall have entire agreement with the Anglican Confession, if only men will weigh its statements, as they ought, in a spirit of zeal, not for party, but for truth.

ARTICULUS XXIII.—*De Vocatione Ministrorum.*

NON licet cuiquam sumere sibi munus publicè prædicandi, aut administrandi Sacramenta in Ecclesia, nisi prius fuerit ad hæc obeunda legitimè vocatus et missus. Atque illos legitimè vocatos et missos existimare debemus, qui per homines, quibus potestas vocandi Ministros atque mittendi in vineam Domini, publicè concessa est in Ecclesia, coaptati fuerint, et adsciti in hoc opus.

PARAPHRASIS. — Est conformis sacræ Scripturæ, doctrinæ sanctorum Patrum, et praxi universalis Ecclesiæ.

ARTICLE XXIII.—*Of Ministering in the Congregation.*

IT is not lawful for any man to take upon him the office of publick preaching, or ministering the Sacraments in the Congregation, before he be lawfully called, and sent to execute the same. And those we ought to judge lawfully called and sent, which be chosen and called to this work by men who have publick authority given unto them in the Congregation, to call and send Ministers into the Lord's vineyard.

EXPLANATION.—This Article is in agreement with Holy Scripture, the doctrine of the holy Fathers, and the practice of the Universal Church.

ARTICULUS XXIV.— *De Precibus Publicis dicendis in lingua vulgari.*

LINGUA populo non intellectâ publicas in Ecclesia Preces peragere, aut Sacramenta administrare, verbo Dei et primitivæ Ecclesiæ consuetudini planè repugnat.

ARTICLE XXIV.—*Of speaking in the Congregation in such a tongue as the people understandeth.*

IT is a thing plainly repugnant to the Word of God, and the custom of the Primitive Church, to have publick Prayer in the Church, or to minister the Sacraments in a tongue not understanded of the people.

PARAPHRASIS.—Scio plerosque ex nostratibus existimare hic decerni, in Scripturis esse præceptum publica Ecclesiæ officia in linguis vernaculis celebrari. Quo nihil minus intenditur D. Paulus enim quem huic articulo hoc astruendi fundamentum fecisse credunt, plane aliud vult. Scribit enim ubi ad Corinthios, apud quos tunc temporis et Hebræos constantissimum fuit in lingua vulgari communia celebrare: non igitur crediderim Paulum Corinthiis imposuisse, aut illud præcipere voluisse, quod jam publicè in usu erat, sed vel de privatis eorum conventibus, vel saltem de privatis colloquiis post communia officia peracta habitis, ibi agit, et eos reprehendit, qui dono linguarum præditi etiam in linguis extraneis tunc loquebantur: sicut si aliquis apud nos in lingua Teutonica, quod ridiculum videretur.

Hunc vero esse sensum D. Pauli non potuit latere conditores Articu-

EXPLANATION.—I know that many of our countrymen consider it is here affirmed that in the Scriptures it is commanded that the public offices of the Church be celebrated in the vernacular language. But this is as far as possible from the intention of Scripture. For St. Paul, whom they believe to have given authority for this Article, asserts this plainly means something else. For he is writing to the Corinthians, among whom at that time, as among the Jews, it was the established custom to celebrate the public offices in the vulgar tongue. I cannot, therefore, believe that St. Paul imposed on the Corinthians, or would have meant to order them to do, that which was already in common use publicly; but that he there speaks either of their private assemblies, or at least of private conferences held after the performance of the public offices; and that he blames those who, having received the gift of tongues, even at these times, spoke in foreign tongues; which was the same thing as though any one among us were to speak in German, which would appear ridiculous.

But it could not have escaped the framers of the Articles, that this was

lorum, et consequenter nec contra tam manifestam veritatem aliquid potuerunt ordinare.

Decernit igitur hic Articulus esse repugnans Scripturis, id est, non doctrinæ Scripturæ, quasi aliquid in oppositum ordinaretur, quod est falsum, ut dictum est; sed scriptioni seu traditioni Scripturæ, quæ fuit apud Corinthios in lingua communi : orationes etiam et administrationes Sacramentorum in Scripturis traditæ, vulgo publica fiebant in lingua communi, quia Scripturæ ipsis in vulgari tradebantur, nam Hebr. Hebræis, Græcè Græcis. Et hoc solum dicit hic Articulus; testatur utique traditionem Scripturæ et omnium ibi contentorum, etiam Sacramentorum, celebratam fuisse in linguis communibus, quod sensu exposito verum est non tamen aliquid hic per modum legis instituitur, vel omnino mandatus, ut in Articulo patet.

Addo, nullam legem dari posse de accidentibus. Per accidens vero est

the meaning of St. Paul; and, consequently, they cannot have meant to affirm anything contrary to such a manifest truth.

This Article, then, asserts that it is repugnant to the Scriptures—that is, not to the doctrine of the Scriptures—as though anything were ordered different to that, which, as we have said, is false; but to the writing or tradition of Scripture which existed at Corinth in the vulgar tongue. The prayers, too, and administrations of the Sacraments handed down in Scripture, were commonly performed in public in the language of the people, because the Scriptures were delivered to them in that language—namely, in Hebrew to the Jews, in Greek to the Greeks, and this alone is asserted by the Article; for it bears witness that the tradition of Scripture, and of all things contained in it, even the Sacraments, was in the vulgar tongue, which in the sense set forth above is true. Nothing, however, here is appointed by way of a law, or at all commanded, as is plain from the Article.

Moreover, no law can be made concerning accidental matters. Now,

quod à singulis in hæc occidentali mundi plaga non intelligatur lingua Latina, quæ per se loquendo est lingua communis ecclesiæ Latinæ; et in hoc ex parte distinguitur à Græcis, unde Græci apud omnes jurisdictioni Patriarchæ Constantinopol. subditos, licet Græci non sint, officia idiomate Græco celebrant: supponitur enim, tam apud Græcos quam Latinos, linguas illas respective communiter addisci, sicut de Latina Beda suo tempore diligenter factitatum testatur. Et hinc Trid. præcipit presbyteris ut parochianos in communibus ecclesiæ officiis instruerent, ut patet fess. 22, c. 8. Unde si dixerimus Paulum vetuisse preces publicas celebrari lingua non communi, intelligi deberet, *nisi adesset qui interpretaretur;* ut recte Articulus V. confessionis Anglicæ sub Edwardo VI. Omnibus ergo modis ecclesiæ satisfacit huic præcepto (si præceptum est), quia interpretem apponunt, in Trident.

Addo ulterius etiam vi hujus Articuli probabiliter inferri posse, de-

it is an accidental matter that some living in the West do not understand the Latin language, which is the common language of the Latin Church, and by this partly is it distinguished from the Greeks; so that the Greeks wherever subject to the jurisdiction of the Patriarch of Constantinople, though they be not Greeks by nation, say their offices in the Greek language; for it is supposed that, among both Greeks and Latins, those languages are respectively learnt by most people, as, in respect of Latin, Bede testifies was sedulously done in his day; and for this reason the Council of Trent (Sess. 22, c. 8) orders priests to instruct their parishioners in the common offices of religion. If, then, we say that St. Paul forbade that public offices should be celebrated except in the vulgar tongue, we must understand, *unless there be some one to interpret;* as was rightly added in the fifth Article under Edward VI. In every respect, then, the Church fulfils this precept (if it be a precept) by ordering interpretation in the Council of Trent.

I add further that, even on the strength of this Article, it may be

bere ecclesiæ officia et Christi Sacramenta in lingua Latina apud nos hodie celebrari; quia per se loquendo (ut dixi) est lingua communis, et communiter intellecta, et publice in singulis' locis edocta; solum autem asseritur in Articulo, quod preces publicæ fiant in lingua a populo intellecta, quod sine dubio intelligi debet de per se, non per accidens loquendo.

Hoc dico, casu quo intelligi contendant Articulum de præsenti usu Ecclesiæ : et ob hanc rationem in Africa, ut testatur Cypr. de Orat. Dom. et Aug. de bono Persev. c. 13, missas et reliqua faciebant Latine, licet lingua vulgaris erat Punica, et Latina ab inferiori plebe non intellecta. De Hispania patet apud Isidorum De Divin. Nomin. et in Concil. Tolet. 4, cap. 2, **12**, 13, 14, 15, et de Anglia nota est historia Bedæ lib. 1, c. 1. Fœminæ quidem rarius intelligebant Latinam, nec de illis intelligi potest Paulus, sed de idiota, id est, de illa cui incumbit respondere, quod non est fœminarum, quæ nec

probably inferred, that the offices of the Church and the Sacraments of Christ ought at the present time to be celebrated amongst us in Latin, because it is, speaking generally, as I said above, the common language and commonly understood, and publicly taught in every place; and it is only asserted in the Article that public prayer should be in a language understood by the people, which ought undoubtedly to be explained of general understanding everywhere, not of accidental variations of language.

I say this in case they should contend that the Article ought to be understood of the present use of the Church. For the reason set forth above, in Africa, as evidenced by St. Cyprian (*de Or. Dom.*) and St. Augustine (*de bon. Persev.*, c. 13), they used to say masses and other offices in Latin, though the common language was the Punic, and Latin was not understood by the lower orders. The same thing is evident as regards Spain from Isidore (*de dic. Nom.*) and the Council of Toledo (4, cap. 2, 12, **13**, 14, 15); and Bede says the same of England (*Hist.* i. 1). Women very seldom

loqui debent in ecclesia, ut ibidem Paulus, et in jure canonico cautum est.

Dices hunc Articulum condemnare ut Scripturæ seu verbo Dei repugnantem, modum ecclesiæ Latinæ celebrantis, sicut etiam Cajet. in 1. ad Cor. 14.

Respondeo me sensum Articuli satis exposuisse; quia tamen communiter sic à Nostratibus intelligitur; referam quid de hoc habeat Cano, l. 5, c. 5, q. 5, *Non auderem asserere esse hæreticum, si aliquis dixerit aliquam ecclesiæ consuetudinem, vel legem esse malam, vel injustam, modo non sint de rebus ad salutem necessariis, quia ut Deus non deficit in necessariis, sic non abundat in superfluis.* Sic ille. Consequentur ad hanc doctrinam, si Nostrates simpliciter dicerent hanc Ecclesiæ legem seu consuetudinem esse malam, cum non videatur saluti necessaria secundam doctrinam à Cano alibi traditam, ipse non eos hæreseos incusaret. *Ecclesia enim mores quosdam à Christo et Apos-*

understood Latin, nor can St. **Paul** be supposed to speak of them; but of the ἰδιώτης—that is, of him who had to respond—which could not be the case with regard to women, who ought not even to speak in church, as St. Paul says in the same place, and as is declared in the Canon law.

It may be said that this Article condemns, as repugnant to Scripture or the Word of God, the manner of celebrating of the Latin Church, as also does Cajetan on 1 Cor. 14.

To which I answer that I have sufficiently set forth the sense of the Article. Since, however, it is thus commonly understood by men of this country, I will quote what Canus says about this (l. 5, c. 5, qu. 5)—"I would not venture to assert that it was heretical, if any one said that any custom of the Church or law was bad or unjust, provided it were not about matters necessary for salvation; because, as God is not wanting in what is necessary, so He does not superabound in what is more than necessary." Consequently, with reference to this doctrine, if our countrymen simply said that this law or custom of the Church was bad, since it does not seem necessary to

tolis traditos retinet, in quibus qui Ecclesiam errare diceret, hic erroris ejus authores Christum et Apostolos faceret: alii vero mores sunt post Apostolos inducti, in quibus quamvis Ecclesia erraret, non propterea fides periclitaretur. Hæc ille. Cujus sententiam, ego non sum tantus, ut condemnare ausim. Adverte tamen, Dicere quod Missa in lingua vulgari tantum celebrari debeat, eo quod sit contra Christi institutionem in Trid. sess. 22, c. 9, anathemati subjicitur. Hoc autem non dicunt *tantum* in lingua vulgari, sed pro ratione audientium: et hinc in aliquibus collegiis, nempe ubi omnes callent **Latinem**, officium divinum hodie sit Latine; nec Missa, sed **precum publicarum** (quæ aliud sunt à Missa) mentionem faciunt. Quod non est contra Trid. directe, quia Trid. solum loquitur de Missa, et quod **tantum** fiat in vulgari, eo quod sit contra Christi institutionem: neutrum tamen horum dicit Articulus, ut ibi patet, sed dum dicit esse repugnans verbo Dei (licet ut ostendi superius, non omnino de hoc agi) intelligi deberent institutioni D. Pauli, non Christi, cujus scripta sub nomine verbi Dei comprehenduntur, omnia

salvation, according to the doctrine elsewhere laid down by Canus, he would not charge them with heresy: "For the Church retains certain customs delivered to her by Christ and the Apostles, in which any one who said that the Church was in error would make Christ and the Apostles the authors of that error; but there are other customs introduced since the Apostles, in which, even if the Church erred, the faith would not therefore be in jeopardy." This is what he says; and I have not such an opinion of myself as to presume to condemn his opinion. To say that Mass ought only to be celebrated in the vulgar tongue, or that the opposite practice is contrary to Christ's institution, is anathematized by the Council of Trent (Sess. 22, c. 9). But this the Article treated of does not say; for it is not said in the vulgar tongue *only*, but with respect to the hearers. For this cause in some colleges, where all are skilled in Latin, the divine office is at this day said in Latin. Nor, again, is Mass spoken of; but public prayer (which is a different thing from the Mass). So that the statement is not directly against the

tamen ab Apostolis demandatur, non sunt mandata Christi, ut ab omnibus concessum est, et consequenter licet dixissent esse contra institutionem Apostoli, non esset expresse contra fidem. De Cajetano quidem, audacter scripsit, sed ante Trid.

Council of Trent, for that speaks of Mass only, and of the opinion that it must by Christ's institution be always said in the vulgar tongue. Neither, however, of these is asserted by the Article, as is plain; but when it says that the practice is repugnant to the Word of God (though as I have shown above it does not treat of this absolutely), it should be understood to mean repugnant to the institution not of Christ but of St. Paul, whose writings are comprised under the name of the Word of God; but all things ordered by the Apostles are not commands of Christ, as is allowed by all; and consequently, though they might have called it against the institution of the Apostle, such a statement would not be expressly against the faith. With regard to Cajetan, indeed, he wrote rashly, but it was before the Council of Trent.

ARTICULUS XXV.—*De Sacramentis.*

SACRAMENTA à Christo instituta, non tantum sunt notæ professionis Christianorum, sed certa quædam potius testimonia, et efficacia signa gratiæ atque bonæ in nos

ARTICLE XXV.—*Of the Sacraments.*

SACRAMENTS ordained of Christ be not only badges or tokens of Christian men's profession, but rather they be certain sure witnesses, and effectual signs of grace, and God's

voluntatis Dei, per quæ invisibiliter ipse in nobis operatur, nostramque fidem in se non solum excitat, verum etiam confirmat.

Duo à Christo Domino nostro in evangelio instituta sunt Sacramenta, scilicet Baptismus, et Cœna Domini.

Quinque illa vulgò nominata Sacramenta, scilicet Confirmatio, Pœnitentia, Ordo, Matrimonium, et Extrema Unctio, pro Sacramentis Evangelicis habenda non sunt, ut quæ partim à prava Apostolorum imitatione profluxerunt, partim vitæ status sunt in Scripturis quidem probati: sed Sacramentorum eandem cum Baptismo, et Cœna Domini rationem non habentes, ut quæ signum aliquod visibile seu ceremoniam à Deo institutam non habeant.

Sacramenta non in hoc instituta sunt à Christo ut spectarentur, aut circumferrentur, sed ut rite illis uteremur, et in iis duntaxat, qui dignè percipiunt, salutarem habent effectum: qui vero indignè percipiunt, damnationem (ut Paulus inquit) sibi ipsis acquirunt.

good will towards us, by the which he doth work invisibly in us, and doth not only quicken, but also strengthen and confirm our faith in him.

There are two Sacraments ordained of Christ our Lord in the Gospel, that is to say, Baptism, and the Supper of the Lord.

Those five commonly called Sacraments, that is to say, Confirmation, Penance, Orders, Matrimony, and Extreme Unction, are not to be counted for Sacraments of the Gospel, being such as have grown partly of the corrupt following of the Apostles, partly are states of life allowed in the Scriptures; but yet have not like nature of Sacraments with Baptism and the Lord's Supper, for that they have not any visible sign or ceremony ordained of God.*

The Sacraments were not ordained of Christ to be gazed upon, or to be carried about, but that we should duly use them. And in such only as worthily receive the same they have a wholesome effect or operation: but they that receive them unworthily purchase to themselves damnation, as Saint *Paul* saith.†

[* "This definition does not exclude Matrimony, Confirmation, Absolution, and **Orders** from being *in some sense* Sacraments; but excludes them from being *such* Sacraments as Baptism and the Communion. . . . Four out of five the Church of England admits, at least in a modified form."—Bp. Harold Browne *On the Articles*, 6th Edition. London: Longmans, 1864.]

[† Dr Harold Browne, Bishop of Ely,

(51)

PARAPHRASIS.—Paragraphus primus et secundus Catholicus est: tertius exponendus. Ubi sciendum, quod receptissima veritas est, tam in Occidentali quam Orientali Ecclesia; septem esse Sacramenta, in quorum administratione, si ex officio fiat (potest esse difficultas aliqua de ministro matrimonii) necessario requiritur homo sacer, ut minister Ecclesiæ; ut conveniunt omnes Doctores, et in Florentino cum liberrimo consensu totius Ecclesiæ definitum fuit, illa esse proprie dicta Sacramenta; et licet Græci in aliquibus aliis punctis, præsertim de absoluto suprematu Papæ resilierint: in hac tamen veritate usque in hodiernum diem constant; ut testantur eorum Scriptores. Ne igitur hæc nostratium censura videatur toti Ecclesiæ repugnare, glossanda est, hic non negari omnem rationem Sacramentis cæteris

EXPLANATION.—The first and second paragraphs are Catholic, the third requires explanation. On this point it must be first understood, that it is a most received truth, as well in the Eastern as in the Western Church, that there are seven Sacraments, in the administration of which, if done by virtue of the administrator's office (there may be some difficulty as to the minister of matrimony), of necessity is required a consecrated person as a minister of the Church; as all the Doctors agree, and as it was defined at Florence with the most free consent of the whole Church, that they are properly called Sacraments; and although the Greeks have gone back on some other points, especially concerning the absolute supremacy of the Pope, they hold to this truth (of the seven Sacraments) up to the

in his *Treatise on the Articles* (p. 582), thus writes regarding Confirmation :—" Confirmation, in the primitive Church, followed immediately on Baptism, and, as above noted, was made ordinarily a part of Baptism. Tertullian and Cyril of Jerusalem both speak of the catechumens as first receiving Baptism, and then immediately on their coming out of the water receiving chrism and imposition of hands," —clear proof enough that, whether Confirmation in the Roman Church be either a " corrupt following of the Apostles," or a " state of life allowed in the Scriptures," the present practice of the Church of England, in which Confirmation is deferred so long, is unquestionably the exact reverse of that " primitive use" of which so much is said. Church-of-England people in this instance, as perhaps in other particulars, need to remember the parable of the mote and the beam.]

E. 2

quinque, quæ ibi specificat, sed solum differentiam ponere, tam in necessitate, quam principalitate Baptismi, et Eucharistiæ, respectu cæterorum, in quo convenit tota Antiquitas, cum universa Schola Theologorum, ut omnibus notum est. Hunc vero esse sensum genuinum hujus articuli, patet, quia subditur (*sed non eandem habent rationem*) non negat ergo simpliciter esse Sacramenta, quod antea dixerat, sed in dissimili gradu, quod ultro concedimus. Fuit quidem olim inter Doctores aliqua controversia, an omnia Sacramenta fuerint à Christo instituta immediatè; de qua re Sotus 4. d. i. q. 5, a. 2, et Durand. d. 2, q. i. putant non esse hæresim dicere Unctionem et Confirmationem non esse instituta à Christo, Favet Hugo 2, de Sacr. p. 15, c. 2, et Bonav. d. 7, a. 1, q. i., sed optime illorum doctrinam oppugnat Doctor 4, d. 2, q. i. Omnes tamen conveniunt esse de fide septem esse Sacramenta.

present day, as their writers bear witness. Lest, however, this censure on the part of our countrymen should seem repugnant to the whole Church, it must be noticed that in this Article some **nature of Sacraments** is not denied to the other five specified, but only a difference is made in the necessity and greater dignity of Baptism and the Eucharist in respect of the rest, with which all antiquity agrees, and the whole theology of the schools, as is known to all. But it is clear that this is the the true sense of this Article, because there is added *have not the like nature;* it does not deny that they are Sacraments at all, which it had before called them, but says that they are so in a different degree, which we readily grant. There was of old a question among the Doctors, "Whether all the Sacraments were ordained of Christ?" On which point Sotus (4 d. 1, qu. 5, a. 2) and Durandus (d. 2, q 1) think it is not heresy to say that **Unction** and **Confirmation** were not **instituted** by Christ. To this opinion incline Hugo (2 *de Sacr.* p. 15, c. 2) and St. Bonaventure (d. 7, a. 1, qu. 1); but the [Subtle] Doctor successfully opposes their doctrine

Alia verba intermixta in Articulo non sunt directe responsiva ad quæsitum, quod erat de numero Sacramentorum, unde secundum regulas Doctorum post Canum l. 5, q. 4, etiam in definitionibus Ecclesiæ, non ligantur Catholici ad **singula verba** definitioni annexa, nec sequaces hujus censuræ, ut etiam jurent in illa **verba per** accidens allata.

Paragraphus ultimus **ponderabitur** in Articulo XXVIII.

ARTICULUS XXVI.—*De vi institutionum divinarum, quod eam non tollat malitia hominum.*

QUAMVIS in Ecclesia visibili, bonis mali semper sint admixti, atque interdum ministerio verbo **et** Sacramentorum administrationi præsint : tamen cum non suo, sed Christi nomine agant, ejusque mandato et authoritate ministrent, illorum ministerio uti licet, cum in verbo **Dei** audiendo, tunc in Sacramentis percipiendis, neque **per illorum** malitiam effectus institutorum Christo tollitur, aut gratia donorum Dei minuitur,

(4 d. 2, qu. 1). All, however, agree that it is of faith that there are seven Sacraments.

The remaining words interspersed with **the Article** have no direct reference to the question, which concerned the number of the Sacraments, so that according to the rules of the Doctors after Canus (l. 5, qu. 4), even in the definitions of the Church, **Catholics are not bound to** every word annexed to the definition, nor are those who accept this censure bound to accept those words accidentally introduced.

The last paragraph will be considered in treating on Article XXVIII.

ARTICLE XXVI.—*Of the Unworthiness of the Ministers, which hinders not the effect of the Sacrament.*

ALTHOUGH in the visible Church the evil be ever mingled with the good, and sometimes the evil have chief authority in the Ministration of the Word and Sacraments, **yet** forasmuch as they do not the same in their own name, but in Christ's, and do minister by his commission and authority, we may use their Ministry, both **in hearing** the Word of God, and **in the** receiving of the Sacraments. **Neither**

quoad eos qui fide et rite sibi oblata percipiunt, quæ propter institutionem Christi et promissionem efficacia sunt, licet per malos administrantur.

Ad Ecclesiæ tamen disciplinam pertinet, ut in malos Ministros inquiratur, accusenturque ab his qui eorum flagitia noverint, atque tandem justo convicti judicio, deponantur.

Paraphrasis.—Est ipsa doctrina Ecclesiæ et omnium Patrum.

is the effect of Christ's ordinance taken away by their wickedness, nor the grace of God's gifts diminished from such as by faith and rightly do receive the Sacraments ministered unto them; which be effectual, because of Christ's institution and promise, although they be ministered by evil men.

Nevertheless, it appertaineth to the discipline of the Church, that enquiry be made of evil Ministers, and that they be accused by those that have knowledge of their offences; and finally being found guilty, by just judgment be deposed.

Explanation.—This is the very doctrine of the Church, and of all the Fathers.

Articulus XXVII.—*De Baptismo.*

BAPTISMUS non est tantum professionis signum ac discriminis nota, qua Christiani à non Christianis discernantur: sed etiam est signum regenerationis, per quod tanquam per instrumentum recte Baptismum suscipientes, ecclesiæ inseruntur, promissiones de remissione peccatorum atque adoptione nostra in filios Dei per Spiritum Sanctum visibiliter obsignantur, Fides confirmatur, et vi divinæ invocationis gratia angetur. Baptismus parvulorum omnino in Ecclesia retinendus est,

Article XXVII.—*Of Baptism.*

BAPTISM is not only a sign of profession, and mark of difference, whereby Christian men are discerned from others that be not christened, but it is also a sign of Regeneration or new Birth, whereby, as by an instrument, they that receive Baptism rightly are grafted into the Church; the promises of the forgiveness of sin, and of our adoption to be the sons of God by the Holy Ghost, are visibly signed and sealed; Faith is confirmed, and Grace increased by virtue of prayer

ut qui cum Christi institutione optime congruat.

PARAPHRASIS.—Idem est judicium.

ARTICULUS XXVIII.—*De Cœna Domini.*

CŒNA Domini non est tantum signum mutuæ benevolentiæ Christianorum inter sese, verum potius est Sacramentum nostræ per mortem Christi Redemptionis. Atque adeo rite digne et cum fide sumentibus, panis quem frangimus est communicatio Corporis Christi: similiter poculum benedictionis est communicatio Sanguinis Christi.

Panis et vini Transubstantiatio in Eucharistia ex sacris literis probari non potest, sed apertis Scripturæ verbis adversatur, Sacramenti na-

unto God. The Baptism of young Children is in any wise to be retained in the Church, as most agreeable with the institution of Christ.

EXPLANATION.—My judgment on this is the same.

ARTICLE XXVIII.—*Of the Lord's Supper.*

THE Supper of the Lord is not only a sign of the love that Christians ought to have among themselves one to another; but rather it is a Sacrament of our Redemption by Christ's death: insomuch that to such as rightly, worthily, and with faith, receive the same, the Bread which we break is a partaking of the Body of Christ; and likewise the Cup of Blessing is a partaking of the Blood of Christ.

Transubstantiation* (or the change of the substance of Bread and Wine) in the Supper of the Lord, cannot be proved by holy Writ; but it is

---

[* "What is here opposed as 'Transubstantiation,' is the shocking doctrine that 'the Body of Christ,' as the Article goes on to express it, is NOT 'given, taken, and eaten after an heavenly and spiritual manner, but is carnally pressed with the teeth;' that It is a body or substance of a certain extension or bulk in space, and a certain figure and due disposition of parts; whereas we hold that the only substance [as] such is the bread which we see. This is plain from Article XXIX., which quotes St. Augustine as speaking of the wicked as 'carnally and visibly pressing with their teeth the *Sacrament* of the Body and Blood of Christ,' not the real substance,—a statement which even the Breviary introduces into the service for Corpus Christi Day."—*Tract* 90, 3rd Edition, p. 47.]

turam evertit, et multarum superstitionum dat occasionem.

Corpus Christi datur, accipitur, et manducatur in Cœna, tantum cælesti et spirituali ratione. Medium autem quo Corpus Christi accipitur et manducatur in Cœna, fides est.

Sacramentum Eucharistiæ ex institutione Christi non servabatur, circumferebatur, elevabatur, nec adorabatur.

PARAPHRASIS. — Primus paragraphus cum omnibus suis cojunctivis affirmative solum, sicut ibi, prolatis, Catholicus est, secundus paragraphus examinandus.

Negare Transubstantiationem divinam in hoc tremendo mysterio est contra veritatem fidei, prout definitum est in Lateranensi et Trid. Scio aliquos universalitatem prioris licet magni Concilii in dubium vocare: scio alios etiam ex nostris infallibili-

repugnant to the plain words of Scripture, overthroweth the nature of a Sacrament, and hath given occasion to many superstitions.

The Body of Christ is given, taken, and eaten, in the Supper, only after an heavenly and spiritual manner. And the mean whereby the Body of Christ is received and eaten in the Supper is Faith.

The Sacrament of the Lord's Supper was not by Christ's ordinance reserved, carried about, lifted up, or worshipped.*

EXPLANATION.—The first paragraph, with all its clauses stated, as there affirmatively only, is Catholic. The second must be examined.

To deny divine Transubstantiation in this tremendous mystery is contrary to the truth of the faith, as it has been defined in the Lateran and Tridentine Councils. I know that some persons have questioned the universality of the former Council, though it was a great one; and I

[* This statement is a mere truism. It might be paralleled thus:—

The Sacrament of Baptism was not by Christ's ordinance celebrated in a church, nor by a minister in a surplice, nor at a font (properly so called).

The Sacrament of Order was not by Christ's ordinance conveyed by a form in which the instruments of the Mass are delivered.

The Sacrament of Penance was not by Christ's ordinance administered in a confessional.

The Sacrament of Holy Matrimony was not by Christ's ordinance administered with the use of a ring.]

tatem Conciliorum Generalium diminuere, quos frequenter citant nostrates. Constans autem doctrina Doctorum est utrique opposita; ut ut est: saltem omnes subscribunt Theoremati octavo Mirandulæ, de fide et ordine credendi: *Determinationibus quæ a Concilio, vel a summo Pontifice fiunt super eis dubitationibus, quæ substantiam fidei concernunt, quoaddum universalis Ecclesia non reclamaret* (id est, prout ipse alibi, tacite vel interpretative consentiret) *necessario credendum est.*

Patet autem apud omnes Theologos, et illorum temporum scriptores, nullibi huic decreto Transubstantiatione fuisse reclamatum, immo saltem tacite fuisse approbatum; nec ab ullo dubitatum, hanc resolutionem ad substantiam fidei pertinere. Et ut ipse Scotus qui liberius reliquis de hoc puncto egit 4. dist. ii. fatetur post solemnem declarationem Ecclesiæ, tenendum esse de substantia fidei. Hic igitur vel nusquam definitio legitime proclamata est, nos vero in Anglia particulariter actis hujus

know that others among ourselves, who are frequently cited in this country, disparage the infallibility of General Councils. The constant opinion of the doctors is, however, opposed to both, and, whatever be the truth, at least all subscribe to the eighth Theorem of Mirandula (*de Fid. et Ord. Credendi*) : " We must of necessity believe the decrees which are made by a Council or by the Sovereign Pontiff, upon those questions which concern the substance of the faith, so long that is as the universal Church does not repudiate them" (that is, as he himself says elsewhere, if the Church tacitly or implicitly consents).

It is, however, clear from all theologians and writers of that date, that this decree on Transubstantiation was no where repudiated, nay, that it obtained at any rate tacit approval; nor has any one doubted that this decision pertained to the substance of the faith. And as Scotus himself, who has treated this point more freely than others (4 dist. ii.), owns, after the solemn declaration of the Church, it must be held to be of the substance of the faith. On this point, then, or on none what-

Concilii consensimus, ut patet in multis textibus Juris nostri municipalis, et in Synodis provincialibus, **ut patet apud Lindwoodum.**

Debet igitur glossari hic Articulus; eos scilicet solum condemnare antiquum errorem Capharnaïtarum, sc. carnalem præsentiam Christi, id est, quasi Christus modo **naturali seu carnali hic existeret, et dentibus** nostris masticetur, prout sonare videtur Canon, *Ego Berengarius*, in Concilio Romano sub Nicolao, et refertur de conseer. d. 2.

Sensus ergo est, quod panis seu **substantia** panis, cum suo modo existendi naturali, **in** substantiam corporis cum suo modo existendi naturali, seu carnali mutaretur, quod omnino repugnat Scripturæ, et destrueret naturam Sacramenti; ut recte in Articulo asseritur, Christus enim tunc carnaliter, seu sensualiter, non sacramentaliter, **et modo spirituali** et ineffabili subesset speciebus seu elementis consecratis, ad Sacramentum enim ut sic, requiritur im-

ever, has a decision been lawfully pronounced, and we in England have in particular consented to the acts of this Council, as is clear in many **texts of our municipal law,** and in our provincial **synods,** as is clear from Lindwood.

This Article ought, then, to be explained thus: that the authors only condemn the old error of the Capharnaïtes, namely, the carnal presence of Christ, that is as though Christ was present in the Sacrament in a natural or carnal manner, and were chewed by the teeth, as seems to be implied by the words of the Canon (*Ego Berengarius*) in the Roman Council under Nicolas I. (*Consec.* d. 2).

The sense, then, is that the bread or substance of bread, with its natural mode of existence, would be changed into the substance of a body, with its natural or carnal mode of existence, which is wholly repugnant to Scripture, and would destroy the nature of a Sacrament, as is rightly asserted in the **Article.** For then Christ would be present under the species **or** consecrated elements in a carnal or sensible manner, not sacramentally. Now for a Sacrament, as

mediatum significatum esse aliquid spirituale in re vel saltem in modo: non enim Sacramenta sunt signa sensibilia, sensibilium vel corporalium significativa, sed effectiva gratiæ insensibilis: non ergo corporis cum suo modo quantitativo, sed modo spirituali subsistentis: gratia enim hic significata, est gratia subsistens, scilicet Corpus Christi primario et formaliter, ut optime Doctor ubi supra.

Error igitur iste pertractus, solum hic condemnatur: iste enim solum adversatur rationi Sacramenti, ut ostensum est; iste etiam solum adversatur Scripturæ, quia illam solam intelligentiam hujus mysterii ut erroneam perstrinxit Christus Dominus, Joan. 6.

Quod autem non negent Transubstantiationem ab Ecclesia definitam, vel ex hoc patet, quia utraque Ecclesia scilicet tam Orientalis, quam Occidentalis, in hoc conveniunt: nec in ullo Concilio fuit de hoc disceptatio inter eos, ut recte observat Arcudius l. 3, c. 2, de Eucharistia

such, is required that the thing immediately signified should be something spiritual, either in itself or at least in the manner of its being, for Sacraments are not sensible signs signifying sensible or corporal things, but effectually conveying insensible grace: so this Sacrament is not the sign of a body in its natural quantitative manner, but of a body subsisting in a spiritual manner, for the grace here signified is the grace forming its substance, namely, the Body of Christ primarily and formally, as the Doctor excellently says (*ubi supra*).

The error alluded to above then, and no more, is condemned in this place, for that alone is repugnant to the nature of a Sacrament, as has been shown, because Christ our Lord has condemned that mode alone of understanding this mystery as erroneous (*St. John* vi.).

But that Transubstantiation as defined by the Church is not denied, is plain even from this, that both the Eastern and Western Churches are agreed upon the doctrine, nor has there ever in any Council been any dispute between them on this point, as is rightly observed by Arcudius

fol. 130. Fuit quidem quæstio in Florentino, quibus verbis facta sit Transubstantiatio, sed nihil aliud. Etiam Hieremias in cap. 10, suæ censuræ contra Lutheranos idem fatetur. Nemo vero dubitat puncta ab utraque Ecclesia credita obligare omnes. Nostrates vero *mutationem, alterationem, transmutationem* nec solum *in effigie* sed *natura*, id est, μετουσίαν, fatentur post sanctos Patres; ut patet apud D. Andrewes contra Perronium, et D. Montacutium, fol. 256. Verum quidem est, quod Suarez tom. 3, quæstione 75, disp. 50, sect. 1, notat hæc verba maxime accedere ad proprietatem mysterii explicandam, et probabilissimum est Patres in illo sensu, hæc verba usurpasse, sed ad majorem claritatem, Ecclesia elegit verbum *transubstantiationis*. *Transmutatio* tamen *in natura*, ut loquantur eorum Doctores, seu μετουσία, in omni sensu Philosophico valde premit hunc Articulum in rigore sermonis sumptum, ubi negat simpliciter mutationem substantiæ panis et vini, quod directe astruit μετουσία Sanc-

(l. 3, c. 2, *de Eucharistia*, fol. 130). There was, indeed, a question at Florence at what words of the office the change took place, but no more. Even Hieremias (*Censur. contr. Lutheran.*, c. 10) allows the same. Now no one doubts but that points believed by both Churches are obligatory upon all men. Writers of this country allow a *change*, an *alteration*, a *transmutation*, and that not only in form but in nature; that is, they confess a change of substance,[*] according to the holy Fathers, as is clear by Dr. Andrewes against Perronius and Dr. Montagu (fol. 256). It is indeed true, as Suarez (tom. 3, qu. 75, disp. 50, § 1) notes, that these words are the fittest for explaining the nature of the mystery, and it is most probable that the Fathers used them in that sense, but for greater distinctness the Church chose the word *Transubstantiation*. But a *transmutation in nature*, or μετουσία, to quote their doctors, according to all philosophy, presses close upon this Article taken in the rigorous meaning of the words, which

---

[*] ["The term transubstantiation (μετουσίωσις) was adopted by the Synod of Bethlehem." — Oxenham's *Catholic Doctrine of the Atonement*. Introduction, p. xliv. London: Longmans, 1865.]

torum Patrum, et *transmutatio in natura* eorum. Necessario igitur recurrendum est ad glossam nostram superius insinuatam.

Paragraphus tertius simul cum primo examinabitur in Articulo sequenti.

Paragraphus ultimus videtur negare omnem adorationem venerabili Sacramento: sed melius inspiciendo, putem ipsos solum excludere adorationem latriæ, ut patet apud D. Andrewes contra Perronium, et D. Juellum in Apol. pro Ecclesia Angliæ, et alios eorum doctores, quod Catholicum sentio; loquendo propriè et per se, sicut Doctor Subt. cum Ovando et omnibus Scotistis, 3, distinctione 9, quæstione 1, negant humanitati Christi latriam per se, immo Doctores communiter ipsis personis divinis præcisè sumptis, id est, sub ratione formali constitutiva personarum, quæ est relatio, negant subesse terminum formalem adorationis latriæ, sed hoc Deitati solum

simply deny the change of the substances of bread and wine, which the μετουσία of the Fathers, and their *transmutation in their nature*, directly imply. Of necessity, then, recourse must be had to our interpretation suggested above.

The third paragraph will be examined, together with the first, in the following Article.

The last paragraph seems to deny all adoration to the venerable Sacrament, but on inspecting it more carefully, I think the authors only exclude the worship of *latria*, as is clear from Dr. Andrewes against Perronius, and Dr. Jewel in *Apol. pro Eccl. Angl.*, and other of their Doctors, which I think Catholic, speaking strictly and absolutely, as the Subtle Doctor, with Ovandus and all the Scotists (3 dist. 9, qu. 1), deny that *latria* is due to the human nature of Christ in itself,[*] nay more, the Doctors commonly deny that the formal worship of *latria* is due to the Divine Persons themselves, as such; that is, by reason of what formally constitutes their personality,

---

[*] [On this subject see a valuable article in the number of the *Ecclesiastic* for September, 1857. London: Masters.]

primo competit; relationibus autem, prout identificantur **cum** essentia; sic humanitati Christi, non per se præcisè, **sed prout suppositatur à Deo, eadem adoratio debetur, sicut Rex cum purpura.** Sic etiam **Vasquez,** 3, parte, disp. 96, fusé. Speciebus vero Sacramentalibus, cum non assumantur in identitatem personæ, sed solum fiant signa sensibilia præsentiæ corporis Christi primario, et per consequentiam Deitatis ejus, non competit latria, nisi dixeris per accidens; **per se vero, et prout** sunt terminus formalis adorationis, non nisi duliæ, et quidem inferioris, ut facile sequitur ex dictis. Unde Trident. sapienter formavit Canonem sextum de Euchar. in hæc verba: *Si quis dixerit in Sacramento Eucharistiæ Christum non esse cultu latriæ etiam externo adorandum, et ideo nec festiva peculiari celebritate venerandum, nec in processionibus secundum laudabilem Ecclesiæ consuetudinem solemniter circumgestandum, Anathema sit.* Nota bene; **non dicit Sacramentum, sed Christum in Sacramento latriâ adorandum.**

namely, relation; but [adoration is due] to the relations, as being identified with [the Divine] substance, and to the humanity of Christ, not strictly in itself, but because it is assumed by God as a royal robe is assumed by a king. **So, too, says** Vasquez (3 part. disp. 96). But to the sacramental species, since they are not assumed into identity of person, but only are made sensible signs of the presence of the body of Christ primarily, and by consequence of His divinity, *latria* is not fitting, except accidentally; but in themselves, and so far as they are the formal end of adoration, they **ought only to receive** *dulia*, and indeed the lower kind of *dulia*, as clearly follows from what has been said. So that the Council of Trent wisely drew up the Sixth Canon on the Eucharist in these words (Sess. 13, Canon 6, *on the Holy Eucharist*): "If any one saith that, in the Sacrament of the Eucharist, **Christ is not to be adored with the worship, even external, of** *latria*, and is consequently neither to be venerated with a special festive solemnity, nor to be solemnly borne about in processions, according to the laudable custom of the Church, let

Additur in Articulo, nec reservari nec circumgestari debet, quantum scilicet est ex Christi institutione. Glossam quidem poscit, hæc non à Christi formaliter mandari, quæ tamen ab Ecclesia rectè institui posset; quam consuetudinem licet reprobarent, non tamen ob hoc anathematizantur in Tridentino quia non ex errore non credendi præsentiam Corporis Christi hoc asserunt. Sic Cano lib. quinto, ca. 5, quæst. 4.

him be Anathema." Observe well that the Canon does not say that the Sacrament, but that Christ in the Sacrament is to be adored with *latria*.

It is added in the Article that the Sacrament is not bound to be reserved nor carried about, so far, that is, as was actually of Christ's institution. This requires the explanation, that those things are not formally commanded by Christ, which may nevertheless be rightly instituted by the Church; and although men disapprove this custom, they are not for this anathematised by the Council of Trent, because they do not do this from the error of not believing the presence of the body of Christ. This is supported by Canus (lib. 5, cap. 5, qu. 4).

Articulus XXIX.—*De manducatione Corporis Christi, et impios illud non manducare.*

IMPII et Fide viva destituti licet carnaliter, et visibiliter (ut Augustinus loquitur) Corporis et Sanguinis Christi Sacramentum dentibus premunt; nullo tamen modo Christi participes efficiuntur; sed potius tantæ rei Sacramentum seu symbolum ad judicium sibi manducant et bibunt.

Article XXIX.—*Of the Wicked which eat not the Body of Christ in the use of the Lord's Supper.*

THE Wicked, and such as be void of a lively faith, although they do carnally and visibly press with their teeth (as Saint *Augustine* saith) the Sacrament of the Body and Blood of Christ, yet in no wise are they partakers of Christ; but rather, to their condemnation, do eat and drink the sign or Sacrament of so great a thing.

PARAPHRASIS.—In hoc Articulo non tam conclusio, quam conclusionis causa consideranda est: intellectus enim decreti cujuscunque, etiam universalis Ecclesiæ, ex principiis et fundamentis quibus innititur, sicut conclusio ex præmissis, depromendus est, secundum illud Hilarii: *Intelligentia dictorum, ex causis est assumenda dicendi, quia non sermoni res, sed rei est sermo subjectus.* Principium vero unicum hujus eorum determinationis, est authoritas Augustini, ut patet in Articulo, qui subinde insinuat, vel saltem insinuare videtur, impios non realiter participare panem Dominum, licet panem Domini, *in Joan. Tract.* 59, id est, Sacramentum Christi, non ipsum Christum, ut loquitur Articulus. Mens igitur Augustini exploranda est. Illam vero non esse mentem Augustini patet, quia August. per panem Domini, non intelliget Eucharistiam, sed panem intinctum, quem Dominus porrexit Judæ, ut satis convincitur ex eo quod (lib. 3, de consensu Evang. c. 1) expresse docet, Joannem in illo c. 13, nihil de Eucharistia dixisse; idque adhuc fit manifestius ex lectione Augustini in Psal. xl. 10, unde sumpsit Evangelista verba, quæ ex-

EXPLANATION.—In this Article it is not so much the conclusion, as the reasons for the conclusion, which require consideration; for the meaning of every decree, even of the universal Church, is to be ascertained from the principles and grounds on which it rests, as a conclusion is gathered from its premises, according to the saying of St. Hilary: "The understanding of what is said is to be gathered from the reasons for speaking, because the matter does not depend on what is said, but what is said depends on the matter." Now the sole principle of this determination of theirs is the authority of St. Augustine, who intimates, or at least seems to intimate, that the wicked do not really partake of the bread which is the Lord, though they do of the bread of the Lord (*in Joan. Tract.* 59), that is, the Sacrament of Christ, but not Christ Himself, as the Article says. The intention, therefore, of St. Augustine must be sought. Now it is clear that that is not the intention of St. Augustine, because St. Augustine by the bread of the Lord does not mean the Eucharist, but the sop which our Lord gave to Judas, as is satisfactorily proved

explicat hic S. **Augustinus,** *qui edebat panes meos, levabat contra me calcaneum suum.* Nam ibi tradit verba illa prædicta esse de Juda, et impleta, cum Dominus dedit illi buccellam intinctam; bis enim refert **Scriptura Dominum** dedisse manu sua discipulis comedendum panem, primo cum dedit panem **consecratum,** seu Eucharistiam; secundo cum dedit Judæ panem intinctum; et docet S. Augustinus per priorem manducationem non fuisse prophetiam Psalmi impletam, quia tunc discipuli panem Domini non manducarunt, sed panem Dominum; at per posteriora fuisse impletam, quia illa panis non erat panis Dominus, sed panis Domini; nam infra aperte docet, Judam percepisse Sacramentum cum aliis discipulis, et illum panem intinctum non fuisse Corpus Christi, ut putant inquit ipse, *quidam negligenter legentes.* Quod autem citat illud Apostoli, *quicumque manducaverit,* etc., id non facit, ut insinuet panem intinctum datum Judæ à Domino esse Eucharistiam, sed argumentatur à minori ad majus, et constat ex eo quod subjungit, si inquit, corripitur qui non dijudicat, hoc est, non discernit à cæteris cibis Dominicum corpus,

from his showing expressly (lib. 3, *de Consens. Evang.* c. 1) that St. John, in ch. xiii., does not speak at all of the Eucharist, and this becomes still more clear from reading St. Augustine on Psalm xl. (*Psalm* xl. 10), whence the Evangelist took those words which St. Augustine here explains, " He that eateth bread with Me, hath lifted up his heel against Me :" for there he says that these words were prophesied of Judas, and fulfilled, when our Lord gave to him the sop after He had dipped it; for the Scripture relates that our Lord twice, with His own hand, gave His disciples bread to eat: first, when He gave them the consecrated bread, or the Holy Eucharist; secondly, when He gave Judas the sop which He had dipped; and St. Augustine teaches that the prophecy of the Psalm was not fulfilled by the first eating, because then the disciples had not eaten the bread of the Lord, but the Bread which was the Lord; but that by the second eating it was fulfilled, for that bread was not the Bread which was the Lord, but the Bread of the Lord: for further on he says that Judas received the Sacrament with the other disciples, and that

F

quomodo non damnatur, qui ad ejus mensam fingens amicum, accedit inimicus? si reprehensione tangitur negligentia conjuvantis, quâ pœnâ percutitur venditor invitantis? Hæc ille, ut optime tradit Perronius, ut vero de hoc magis constare possit; audiamus ipsum alibi frequenter hanc veritatem edocentem, epistol. ad Jul. 3, et de Salutaribus Documentis. *Unusquisque antequam corpus Domini nostri Jesu Christi accipiat, seipsum probet, et secundum Apostoli præceptum, sic de pane illo edat, et de calice bibat, quia qui indigne manducat et bibit, judicium sibi manducat et bibit.* Ecce secundum Apostolum, asserit malos ipsum Christi corpus sumere. Etiam de verbis Domini, secundum Matth. serm. ii. *Ad eum modum boni et mali manducant corpus et sanguinem Domini.* Ex quibus, et aliis apud eum tam perspicuis locis, non potest dubitari de mente ejus. Ad sensum igitur Augustini explicandus est hic Articulus, quia nititur soli ejus authoritati, secundum regulam quam dedi in initio, vel dicendum ad hunc articulum, sicut Bellar. ad August. Scil., impios non Dominum, id est, ut Dominum (quia non gratiam Domini), in perceptione

that sop was not the Body of Christ, as, says he, *some who read carelessly* think. Further, in citing that passage of the Apostle, "Whosoever shall eat this bread of the Lord unworthily," &c. (1 *Cor.* xi. 27, 29), he does not imply that the sop given by our Lord to Judas was the Eucharist, but he is arguing from the less to the greater, as is plain from what he adds: If, says he, he is reproved who does not discern, that is, does not distinguish the Lord's Body from other food, how can he escape condemnation, who being an enemy comes to His Table feigning to be a friend? If the carelessness of the guest is visited with rebuke, with what punishment shall the seller of his host be smitten? Such are his words, as is well set forth by Perronius; but that we may be more certain on this point, let us hear himself elsewhere frequently teaching this truth (*Epist. ad Jul.* 3 *et de salutar. docum.*):—" Let every man, before he receive the Body of our Lord Jesus Christ, examine himself, and, according to the Apostle's precept, let him so eat of that bread and drink of that cup, for he who eateth and drinketh unworthily eateth

Sacramenti sumere; alias ipsum Dominum ibi velatum, secundum Augustinum (ut ostendi) et veritatem fidei, omnes recipiunt. Et ratio ipsa hoc convincit. Non enim *populus communicans, sed sacerdos consecrans*, actione divina, modo quidem ineffabili, huc adducit Corpus Domini; alias laïcis, non Apostolis, tradita fuisset potestas consecrandi, vel saltem utrique simul, quod in schola Christi hactenus inauditum est.

and drinketh judgment to himself." Plainly following the Apostle, he asserts that the wicked receive the very Body of Christ. So, too, on our Lord's words according to St. Matthew (Serm. ii.) :—" In that manner the good and bad together eat the Body and Blood of our Lord." From which passages and others no less clear there can be no doubt as to what was St. Augustine's mind. This Article must then be explained according to St. Augustine's meaning, as it relies on his authority alone, according to the rule which I laid down at the commencement; or we must say with respect to this Article, as Bellarmine does upon St. Augustine, that the wicked receive not the Lord, that is, as the Lord (because they receive not the grace of the Lord), in partaking of this Sacrament; in other respects all receive our Lord there under a veil, according to St. Augustine (as I have shown), and the true faith. And reason itself proves this, for not *the people who communicate but the priest who consecrates*, by a divine operation, in an ineffable manner, brings hither the body of our Lord, else would the power of consecrating

ARTICULUS XXX.—*De utraque specie.*

CALIX Domini laïcis non est denegandus, utraque enim pars Dominici Sacramenti ex Christi institutione et præcepto omnibus Christianis ex æquo administrari debet.

PARAPHRASIS.—Licet *non ex sermone illo apud Joan. 6, recte colligitur, utriusque speciei communionem à Domino præceptam esse: utcunque juxta varias sanctorum Patrum et Doctorum interpretationes intelligatur,* ut recte Trid. sess. 21, can. 5, ponendo tamen fuisse tunc de hoc traditum præceptum, ut asserit Articulus, solum sequitur, per se loquendo, debere singulis utramque speciem conferri; cum quo bene stat, quod ratione circumstantiarum, verbi gratiâ, personæ, loci, vel temporis, possit unica specie sacra synaxis celebrari; nec alia est hodierna praxis Ecclesiæ. Quod autem hoc præceptum (si omnino præceptum est) intelligi debeat accommodatè ad personas seu circumstantias prædictas, ut etiam insinuat

have been given to lay people, not to the Apostles, or at least to both alike, which has hitherto been unheard of in the school of Christ.

ARTICLE XXX.—*Of both kinds.*

THE Cup of the Lord is not to be denied to the Lay-people: for both the parts of the Lord's Sacrament, by Christ's ordinance and commandment, ought to be ministered to all Christian men alike.

EXPLANATION.—Although "it is not rightly gathered from the discourse in *St. John* vi. that the communion of both species was enjoined by the Lord; however, according to the various interpretations of Holy Fathers and Doctors it be understood," as is rightly said in the Council of Trent (sess. 21, can. 5), yet in laying down that there then was a command given on this point, as the Article asserts, it only follows, speaking strictly, that both kinds ought to be administered to each communicant, with which it is quite consistent that, on account of circumstances, for instance, of persons, place, or time, Holy Communion should be administered under one kind, nor is the present custom of

Maldonatus in 6 Joan. patet, quia in primis 600 annis, secundum doctrinam Augustini et Innoc. ministrabatur Eucharistia parvulis recenter baptizatis, non tamen nisi unica specie, scil. Sanguinis, ob difficultatem deglutiendi, ut testatur post alios Hugo de S. Victore de Sacramentis, l. 1, c. 20. Rationi ergo personæ accommodabatur præceptum; rationi vero temporis, sicut ob persecutionem, populus gestabat, et retinebat domi Hostiam consecratam, ut testantur veteres cum Basilio in ep. ad Cæsariam Patritiam; rationi loci, sicut eremitæ ob nimiam distantiam ab Ecclesiis et publicis conventibus Christianorum, aliquando ad annum reservabant Hostiam consecratam, ut ibidem patet apud Basilium et alios.

Ex quibus apertissime constat, Ecclesiam *pro re nata* frequenter unam vel alteram speciem laïcis dis-

the Church more than this. Further, it is clear that this precept (if it be a precept) ought to be understood with accommodation to persons or circumstances as mentioned above (as is suggested by Maldonatus *in Joan.* vi.), because for the first six hundred years, according to SS. Augustine and Innocent, the Holy Eucharist was administered to infants just baptized, under one kind only, namely the Blood, on account of the difficulty in swallowing, as is witnessed, after others, by Hugh of St. Victor (*de Sacr.*, l. i., c. 20). The precept, therefore, was modified in regard of the person; in regard of time, as when on account of persecution, the people carried away the consecrated Host, and kept It at home, as the ancients testify with St. Basil (*Ep. ad Cæsariam Patritiam*); in regard of place, as when the hermits, on account of their great distance from churches and public assemblies of Christians, sometimes reserved the consecrated Host for a year, as is mentioned in the same place by St. Basil, and by others.

From which cases it most plainly appears, that the Church upon occasion frequently administered one or

tribuisse; nec aliud in Constant. Basiliens. vel Trid. cautum est, nec aliud dicit hic Articulus.

Dices, quicquid sit de rigore sermonis in Articulo, saltem frequenter à Nostratibus exponi, quasi redargueret modernam praxim Ecclesiæ.

Respondeo, quod Cano, lib. 5, quæst. 4, excusat ab hæresi eum qui affirmaret Ecclesiam errare in more communicandi plebem sub una specie tantum; et quia Constantiense statuit eos hæreticos qui hoc dicunt, respondet Ecclesiam tunc fuisse sine capite, nec Martinus quintus approbans Concilium, simpliciter approbat illum Articulum, sed solum definit eos qui docuerint Ecclesiam in hujusmodi consuetudine errare, esse vel hæreticos, vel ut sapientes hæresim, condemnandos. Addit: Quod ergo Mart. Concilio præsidens non est ausus nomine hæreseos condemnare, id ego graviori censura, accusare non audeo, nec debeo. Quod si in more ad salutem necessario, qualis ille videtur esse, de quo in Concilio Constant. erat controversia; tanta fuit

the other kind to the laity, nor was anything else provided for by the Councils of Constance, Basle, or Trent, nor does this Article make any different statement.

An objection may be made, that whatever may be strictly implied by the force of the words in the Article, at least it is frequently explained in this country, as condemning the present practice of the Church.

To this I answer that Canus (lib. v., cap. 5, q. 4) excuses from heresy any one who should affirm that the Church erred, in her custom of communicating the people under one kind alone; and with respect to the Council of Constance having decreed that those who assert this are heretics, I reply that the Church was then without a head, nor did Martin V., in approving of the Council, absolutely approve that Article, but only defines that those who shall teach that the Church errs in this custom, are either heretics, or to be condemned as savouring of heresy. He adds: That, then, which Martin, presiding over the Council, did not venture to condemn under the name of heresy, that I neither venture nor have any right to condemn with a

Martini modestia, quanto nos modestiores esse opportet in aliis erroribus condemnandis, qui consuetudini Ecclesiæ minime ad salutem necessariæ repugnantur. Subdit: Atque hæc eadem fortasse causa Martinum V. impulit, ut qui reprehenderent ecclesiasticam illam consuetudinem impartiendi Eucharistiam populo sub una specie, eos non ut hæreticos, sed ut sapientes hæresim condemnarit; cum enim sub utraque olim specie, plebs Sacramentum Eucharistiæ acceperit, idque Apostoli authoritate, et usu confirmata, non erat hæreticum in dubium vertere, an vetus ille Ecclesiæ mos novo esset præferendus, sed Wiclefistæ idcirco asserebant Ecclesiam errare, quia existimabant necessariam esse plebi ad salutem, utramque Sacramenti speciem sumere, huc detorquentes illa Domini verba, *Nisi manducaveritis,* etc. Prudentissime Martinus quintus vituperationem ecclesiastici novi moris, non dixit esse, sed hæresim sapere. Hæc ille. Et certo non levis est maculæ, hæresim sapere.

heavier censure. But if in a moral question necessary to salvation, such as that seems to be, which was the subject of controversy at the Council of Constance, the moderation of Martin was so great, how much more moderate ought we to be in condemning other errors which oppose a custom of the Church in a matter not at all necessary to salvation. He then adds: And perhaps this same cause moved Martin V. to condemn those who attacked that ecclesiastical custom of administering the Eucharist to the people under one kind, not as heretics, but as savouring of heresy; for, since of old the people used to receive the Sacrament of the Eucharist under both kinds, and this was established by the authority of the Apostle and by custom, it was not heretical to raise a doubt whether that ancient custom of the Church was to be preferred to the new; but the Wiclifites asserted that the Church had erred on this point, because they thought that it was necessary for salvation for the people to receive both kinds of the Sacrament, perverting to this meaning those words of our Lord: "Except ye eat the Flesh of the Son of

Sunt quidem duo Canones de hoc in Tridentino sess. de Communione, c. 1. *Si quis dixerit ex Dei præcepto, vel necessitate salutis omnes et singulos Christi fideles utramque speciem sanctissimi Eucharistiæ Sacramenti sumere debere, Anathema sit.* Can. 2. *Si quis dixerit, sanctam Ecclesiam Catholicam non justis causis, et rationibus adductam fuisse, ut laicos, atque etiam clericos non conficientes, sub panis tantum modo specie communicaret, aut in eo errasse, Anathema sit.*

Gravissimus Cano non potuit ignorare hos Canones, qui interfuit Tridentino, et can. 6, de Eucharistia ibidem citat; tamen resolvit solum sapere hæresin, dicere Ecclesiam in illa nova consuetudine errare, judicium de hac ejus doctrina penes doctiores sit.

Man, and drink His Blood," &c. Most prudently, then, did Martin V. say that blaming the new ecclesiastical custom was, not heresy, but savouring of heresy. Such is his statement. And certainly it is no light stain to savour of heresy.

Now there are two canons of the Council of Trent on this point. (Sess. xxi. *de Commun.*, can. 1): "If any one saith, that by precept of God, or necessity of [to] salvation, all and each of the faithful of Christ ought to receive both species of the most holy Sacrament of the Eucharist, let him be anathema." Can. ii.: "If any one saith that the Holy Catholic Church was not induced by just causes and reasons to communicate under the species of bread only laymen, and also clerics when not consecrating, let him be anathema."

The most learned Canus cannot have been ignorant of these canons, who was present in the Council of Trent, and quotes in the same passage the sixth canon "On the Eucharist;" yet he decides that it only savours of heresy, to say that the Church errs in that new custom: let the decision on this opinion of his rest with more learned men.

Ego tamen quoad casum nostrum, dicerem confessionem Anglicam in neutro Canone percelli; nam quoad primum Canonem, non dicunt esse sic à Deo præceptum, quod sit de necessitate salutis, vel quod non sit accommodate intelligendum ad circumstantias, et cetera. Quod solum in Trident. rejicitur (ut vel maxime patet). Quoad secundum Canonem nullatenus tangunt.

I, however, as far as our subject is concerned, should say that the Anglican Confession falls under the censure of neither canon, for as respects the former canon, it does not assert that communion in both kinds was so commanded by God, as that it is necessary to salvation, or that it may not be understood as capable of accommodation to circumstances, &c., which assertion alone is rejected by the Council (as is most evident). As respects the second canon, it is not in any respect offended against.

ARTICULUS XXXI.— *De unica Christi oblatione in Cruce perfecta.*

OBLATIO Christi semel facta, perfecta est redemptio, propitio, et satisfactio pro omnibus peccatis totius mundi tam originalibus quam actualibus. Neque præter illam unicam est ulla alia pro peccatis expiatio: unde Missarum Sacrificia, quibus vulgo dicebatur sacerdotem offerre Christum in remissionem pœnæ aut culpæ pro vivis et defunctis, blasphema figmenta sunt et perniciosæ imposturæ.

PARAPHRASIS.—Totus hic Arti-

ARTICLE XXXI.—*Of the one Oblation of Christ finished upon the Cross.*

THE Offering of Christ once made is that perfect redemption, propitiation, and satisfaction, for all the sins of the whole world, both original and actual; and there is none other satisfaction for sin, but that alone. Wherefore the sacrifices of Masses, in the which it was commonly said, that the Priest did offer Christ for the quick and the dead, to have remission of pain or guilt, were blasphemous fables, and dangerous deceits.

EXPLANATION.— The whole of

culus durissimus videtur; rectius tamen introspiciendo, non adeo veritati discordem judicem.

Prima pars quoad affirmativa, indubitata est; ubi vero subdit negationem omnis satisfactione pro reatu peccatorum, excepta Christi oblatione in Cruce: intelligi debet, illud totum alteri negari quod in prioribus verbis Christo attributum est: id est, quod nemo præter Christum per quamcumque actionem vel passionem peccata diluere potest, scilicet præscindendo Christum.

In verbis posterioribus, si sobrie intelligantur, nihil agitur contra Sacrificia Missa in se, sed contra vulgarem vel vulgatam opinionem de ipsis, scilicet quod sacerdotes in Sacrificiis offerrent Christum pro vivis et defunctis, in remissionem pœnæ et culpæ, adeo ut virtute hujus Sacrificii ab eis oblati independenter à Crucis Sacrificio, mererentur populo remissionem, etc. Hæc est vulgata opinio, quam hic perstringit Articulus. Cæterum dicendo cum sanctis Patribus in Missa esse vere Sacrificium, licet loquendo secundum sensum veterum Sacrificiorum, non adeo pro-

this Article seems most difficult, but by looking into it more correctly, I should not consider it very dissonant from the truth.

The commencement, so far as it is affirmative, is indubitably true; where, however, there follows a denial of all satisfaction for the guilt of our sins, except the oblation of Christ on the Cross, it must be understood, that the whole of what is attributed to Christ in the first words is denied to any one else; that is, that no one besides Christ can by any action or suffering wash away sin.

In the latter part, if it be understood fitly, nothing is said against the Sacrifice of the Mass in itself, but against the vulgar and commonly-received opinion about it, namely, that priests in this Sacrifice offer Christ for the living and the dead, for remission of pain and guilt, so that by virtue of this Sacrifice offered for them, independently of the Sacrifice of the Cross, they gain remission for the people, &c. This is the popular opinion which the Article here condemns. But it must be said with the Holy Fathers that in the Mass there is a true

priè quia non immolatur modo cruento, sicut in aliis: nam ut habetur in Niceno Canone, *Agnus qui supra sacram Mensam absque immolatione à sacerdotibus immolatur, id est ipse Christus, sacrificatur, licet non iterum mactetur.*

Dicendo etiam (ob hunc Articulum) quod non est propitiatorium primo, quia hoc competit Sacrificio in Cruce, licet bene per se, et quasi secundo, quia principaliter per applicationem Sacrificii cruenti, et per commemorationem ejus, adeo ut ratio propitiationis originaliter Sacrificio in Cruce competat, et illinc, seu virtute illius, hinc, ut etiam recte notavit Cano in locis, l. 12, ca. 12, ubi dicit, satis ut vere et proprie sit Sacrificium, quod mors ita nunc ad peccati remissionem applicetur, ac si nunc Christus moreretur; ubi rationem propitiationis applicationi mortis Christi tribuit: et ad eundem sensum citat Gregorium: *In seipso immortaliter vivens, iterum in hoc mysterio moritur.* Mors igitur incruenta in altari, virtutem suam derivat à morte

Sacrifice, though, if we speak of it in the same sense as the ancient sacrifices, it is not so properly a Sacrifice, for it is not immolated in bloody manner, as in the old; for, as is said in the Nicene Canon, "The Lamb which without immolation is immolated by the priests on the Holy Table, that is Christ Himself, is sacrificed, though It be not again slain."

We must say again (on account of this Article) that it is not primarily propitiatory, for this pertains to the Sacrifice on the Cross, though it may well be called so in itself, and as it were secondarily, because chiefly by the application of the bloody Sacrifice and by commemoration of it; so that propitiation originally belongs to the Sacrifice on the Cross, and from that, or by virtue of that, to this Sacrifice, as Canus has rightly remarked (*Loci Theol.*, lib. xii., cap. 12), where he says that it is sufficient to cause it [the Holy Eucharist] to be truly and properly a Sacrifice, that Christ's death should be so applied for the remission of sin, as if Christ were to die again, where he attributes propitiation to the application of Christ's

cruenta in Cruce, nam ut loquitur Tridentinum, sessione 22, can. secundo de Sacrificio Missæ: *Oblationis cruentæ fructus per hanc uberrime percipiuntur*. Et in hoc sensu hoc Sacrificium est imago et exemplar alterius in Cruce, unde omnis salus radicaliter emanavit. Nulla prorsus hic erit difficultas cum doctioribus Protestantibus, qui plane hoc totum fatentur; ut videre est apud D. Andreros contra Perronium, et D. Montacutium contra Heigham: et alios frequenter; denique nec.

death, and cites St. Gregory to the same purpose. " Living in Himself in immortality, He dies again in this mystery." The unbloody death on the altar, then, derives its virtue from the bloody death upon the Cross; for, as the Council of Trent says (Sess. xxii., cap. 2, *de Sacrific. Miss.*): "The fruits of the bloody oblation are received most plentifully through this [unbloody one]. And in this sense this Sacrifice is an image and setting forth of that Sacrifice upon the Cross, whence, as from a root, all salvation sprung. There will be no difficulty whatever on this point with the more learned Protestants, who allow the whole of this, as is to be seen in Dr. Andrewes against Perronius, and Dr. Montagu against Heigham, and in other writers commonly; nor does this article in any degree gainsay this opinion.

Dicendum tamen (ut dixi) esse etiam per se propitiatorium, quia secundum sanctos Patres est idem Sacrificium, unde Chrysostom, homilia 17, in 10, ad Hebræos: *Nos aliud Sacrificium non facimus quotidie sed semper idem*. Addit: *Immo hujus Sacrificii memoriam facimus*. Non

It must not be said, however (as I said), that this Sacrifice is of itself propitiatory, because, according to the Holy Fathers, it is the same Sacrifice as that on the Cross; as St. Chrysostom says (hom. 17, *in Heb.* x.): "We do not offer a different Sacrifice every day, but always the

ergo solum memorativum, sed simul memoratum ipsum Sacrificium quod in Cruce, licet in modo et aliis circumstantiis differat. Unde ibidem : *Id ipsum offerimus, ne nunc quidem alium agnum, crastina alium, sed semper eundem : ipsum proinde unum est Sacrificium.* Hæc ille. Nec hoc adversatur Articulo, ut patet in glossa, quam opposuimus, nec ipsis Doctoribus ; cum enim ipsi fateantur in Ecclesia esse sacerdotes, esse etiam Sacrificia propitiatoria, fateantur necesse est. Nam ad Hebr. 5 : *Omnis sacerdos constituitur, ut offerat dona et Sacrificia pro peccatis.* Hic igitur necessario pax. Ad pacem vero hanc altius stabiliendam, examinemus naturam Sacrificii ut sic.

Quod à theologis in hunc modum definiri solet. *Sacrificium est actio externa, qua res corporea aliqua et sensibilis à legitimo ministro ritu de-*

same." He adds: "In truth we make a memorial of this Sacrifice." It is not, therefore, merely a commemorative Sacrifice, but the very Sacrifice, too, of the Cross which is commemorated, though it differs in manner and circumstances. "Whence," he says, in the same place, "we offer the very same thing, not at one time one Lamb, at another time another, but always the same; it is entirely one Sacrifice." These are his words. Nor does this contradict the Article, as is plain from the explanation which we have given ; nor the Doctors themselves ; for since they themselves confess that there are priests in the Church, they must necessarily allow that there are also propitiatory Sacrifices. For in Heb. v., it is said that " Every priest is ordained that he may offer both gifts and sacrifices for sins." So that here there must of necessity be reconciliation. But that this peace may be established more firmly, let us examine the nature of sacrifice as such.

Sacrifice is ordinarily defined among theologians in the following manner :—" Sacrifice is an external action, whereby any sensible corporal

bito ac mystico, soli Deo offertur, et in finem congruentem consecratur et transmutatur. Origo litis, si quæ est, consistit in duobus posterioribus punctis: scilicet in consecratione et transmutatione; quid scilicet consecretur, et transmutetur.

Bellar. putat panem consecrari, et Corpus Christi destrui; alii ut Suarez, quod consecratur Corpus Christi, quia offertur et Deo dicatur, destruitur vero, quia vero, licet mystice et incruente, immolatur Christus.

Tandem addit Suarez non est de ratione Sacrificii destructionem seu immutationem rei oblatæ, quod etiam probat ex Levitici vigesimo tertio, ubi erat verum Sacrificium sine mutatione, et hinc totam rationem formalem Sacrificii competere huic.

Ut verum fatear, res est explicatu difficilis: aliquam tamen transmutationem hic fieri, est communius et verius, et hanc requiri, saltem ad Sacrificium pro peccatis, fere omnes

matter is offered to God alone, with a proper and mystical rite by a lawful minister, and is consecrated and changed unto a fitting end." The origin of the controversy, if any exists, is in the two latter points, namely, in the consecration and transmutation; what, that is, is consecrated, and what is changed.

Bellarmine thinks that the bread is consecrated, and the Body of Christ destroyed; others, as Suarez, that the Body of Christ is consecrated, because it is offered and presented to God; and is destroyed, because Christ is immolated truly, though in a mystical and unbloody manner.

Lastly, Suarez adds that the destruction or change of the thing offered is not essential to the idea of Sacrifice, which, too, he proves from Leviticus xxiii., where was a true Sacrifice, without any change, and hence he thinks that the whole formal idea of a Sacrifice is applicable to this.

To own the truth, the matter is difficult to explain; but that some change is made in a Sacrifice is more common and more true an opinion; and that this is required

tenent, quibus etiam conveniunt Protestantes. Sed an illa transmutatio debeat esse cruenta, vel an sufficiat incruenta, videtur esse aliqualis.

Stricte tamen loquendo propter Sacrificium in Cruce, et cætera Sacrificia, quæ communiter cruenta erant, putant Sacrificium Missæ non habere usquequaque eandem rationem Sacrificii : non negant tamen esse Sacrificium (ut dixi) licet non proprie, eo scilicet modo quo illa quia non modo cruento, quod nos ultro dabimus. Est igitur Sacrificium, sed cum termino illo restrictivo à Patribus usurpatum, incruentum, quod non negant.

at least in a sacrifice for sin, almost all theologians hold, with whom Protestants, too, agree. But whether that change ought to be bloody, or whether it would suffice if unbloody, seems to be somewhat controverted.

But to speak strictly, in consequence of the Sacrifice on the Cross and the other Sacrifices, which were commonly bloody, they think that the Sacrifice of the Mass has not altogether the same nature of a Sacrifice; they do not, however, deny that it is a Sacrifice (as I said), though not properly so; that is, not in the same manner as those former Sacrifices, because not in a bloody manner, which we readily grant. It is, therefore, a Sacrifice, but with that restrictive term used by the Fathers, *i.e.*, an unbloody sacrifice, which is not denied by them.

ARTICULUS XXXII.—*De Conjugio Sacerdotum.*

EPISCOPIS, Presbyteris, et Diaconis nullo mandato divino præceptum, ut aut cœlibatum voveant, aut à matrimonio abstineant : licet igitur etiam illis, ut cæteris omnibus Christianis, ubi hoc ad pie-

ARTICLE XXXII.—*Of the Marriage of Priests.*

BISHOPS, Priests, and Deacons, are not commanded by God's Law, either to vow the estate of single life, or to abstain from marriage; therefore it is lawful also for them, as for all other Christian men,

tatem magis facere judicaverint, pro suo arbitratu matrimonium contrahere.

PARAPHRASIS.—Hic Articulus nihil superaddit Articulo XXXI. sub Edvardo VI. paulo quidem explicatius idem declarat, scilicet Episcopis, Presbyteris, et Diaconis non esse mandatum ut cœlibatum voveant: neque jure divino coguntur matrimonio abstinere, et consequenter quantum ad jus divinum, licite et valide possunt nuptias contrahere; quæ est communior opinio scholarum contra nostrum doctissimum Medina, De sacrorum hominum continentia; nec plus hic asseritur, posteriora enim verba non aliud specificant.

ARTICULUS XXXIII.—*De Excommunicatis vitandis.*

QUI per publicam Ecclesiæ denunciationem rite ab unitate Ecclesiæ præcisus est et excommunicatus, is ab universa fidelium multitudine, donec per pœnitentiam publice reconciliatus fuerit arbitrio judicis competentis, habendus est tanquam Ethnicus et Publicanus.

to marry at their own discretion, as they shall judge the same to serve better to godliness.

EXPLANATION.—This Article adds nothing to Article XXXI. under Edward VI., but declares the same thing somewhat more fully, namely, that there is no command binding Bishops, Priests, and Deacons to make a vow of celibacy; nor are they by God's law obliged to abstain from matrimony, and, consequently, as far as God's law goes, they can lawfully and validly contract marriages, which is the more common opinion of the schools, in opposition to the very learned Medina On the Celibacy of the Clergy; nor is more asserted here, for the concluding words specify nothing else.

ARTICLE XXXIII.—*Of excommunicate Persons, how they are to be avoided.*

THAT person which by open denunciation of the Church is rightly cut off from the unity of the Church, and excommunicated, ought to be taken of the whole multitude of the faithful, as an Heathen and Publican, until he be openly reconciled by penance, and received into the Church by a Judge that hath authority thereunto.

PARAPHRASIS.—Hic Articulus Catholicus est, et tam pactis Scripturis quam Antiquitati consonans.

EXPLANATION.—This Article is Catholic, and agreeable both to Holy Scripture and Antiquity.

ARTICULUS XXXIV.—*De Traditionibus Ecclesiasticis.*

ARTICLE XXXIV.—*Of the Traditions of the Church.*

TRADITIONES atque ceremonias easdem non omnino necessarium est esse ubique, aut prorsus consimiles: nam et variæ semper fuerunt, et mutari possunt pro regionum, temporum, et morum diversitate, modo nihil contra verbum Dei instituatur. Traditiones et ceremonias Ecclesiasticas quæ cum verbo Dei non pugnant, et sunt authoritate publica institutæ et probatæ, quisquis privato consilio volens et data opera publice violaverit, is, ut qui peccat in publicum ordinem Ecclesiæ, quique lædit authoritatem magistratus, et qui infirmorum fratrum conscientias vulnerat, publice, ut cæteri timeant, arguendus est.

IT is not necessary that Traditions and Ceremonies be in all places one, and utterly like; for at all times they have been divers, and may be changed according to the diversities of countries, times, and men's manners, so that nothing be ordained against God's Word. Whosoever through his private judgment, willingly and purposely, doth openly break the traditions and ceremonies of the Church, which be not repugnant to the Word of God, and be ordained and approved by common authority, ought to be rebuked openly, (that others may fear to do the like,) as he that offendeth against the common order of the Church, and hurteth the authority of the Magistrate, and woundeth the consciences of the weak brethren.

Quælibet Ecclesia particularis sive nationalis, authoritatem habet instituendi, mutandi aut abrogandi ceremonias, aut ritus Ecclesiasticos, humana tantum authoritate institutos: modo omnia ad ædificationem fiant.

Every particular or national Church hath authority to ordain, change, and abolish, ceremonies or rites of the Church ordained only by man's authority, so that all things be done to edifying.

PARAPHRASIS.—Manifestum est

EXPLANATION.—It is clear that

hic solum **agi** de Traditionibus non doctrinalibus: asserit enim hic **Articulus**, eas secundum circumstantias temporum et locorum, subinde variari posse: quod de doctrina certo tradita per Apostolos, Christianorum nemo asseruit.

Totus igitur hic Articulus mihi verissimus et praxi Ecclesiæ consonans videtur.

Fuisse vero aliqua doctrinalia per **Apostolos** non scripto, sed verbo **posteris tradita** eleganter declarat **Dionys. Areopag.**: Ἐκ νοὸς εἰς νοῦν διὰ μέσου λόγου σωματικοῦ, ἀλλ' ὅμως γραφῆς ἐκτός. Id est, ex animo in animum sine **literis, medio intercedente verbo**, ait fuisse transfusa.

August. etiam, lib. 5 de Baptismo contra **Donatistas**, c. 23, respondens Epistolæ Cypriani ad Pompeium. *Apostoli*, inquit, **nihil** *quidem inde præceperunt, sed consuetudo illo quæ opponebatur Cypriano, ab eorum traditione exordium sumpsisse credenda est, sicut sunt multa quæ universa tenet Ecclesia, et ob hoc ab Apostolis præcepta bene* **creduntur,** *quamvis scripta non reperiantur.*

the Traditions here treated of are not doctrinal, for the Article asserts that they may be changed according to circumstances of times and places, which no Christian ever asserted of doctrine certainly handed down by the Apostles.

The whole Article, therefore, appears to me most true, and agreeable to the practice of the Church.

That there were certain matters of doctrine delivered by the Apostles, not in writing but orally, to their successors, is elegantly expressed by St. Dionysius, the Areopagite. "From mind to mind, by means of bodily speech, but at the same time without writing," he says that matters were transmitted.

St. Augustine also (lib. v., *de Bapt. Cont. Donat.*, c. 23), answering the Epistle of St. Cyprian to **Pompeius, says**: "The Apostles ordered nothing on that point; but that custom, which was opposed by Cyprian, must be believed to have sprung from their tradition, as are many things which the Universal Church holds, and for this reason they are well believed to be ordered by the Apostles, though they be not found in writing."

Et superius, lib. 2, c. 9, dixit: Consuetudinis robore tenebatur orbis terrarum, et *hæc solum opponebatur* inducere volentibus novitatem. Sed de hujusmodi hic non agitur. Quod autem additur in ultimo articulo, verissimum est, et tradit August. in ep. 86, ad Casulanum, et in epist. 119, ad Januarium, et tandem habetur, 31 dist. cap. Quoniam, etc. et cap. Aliter, et est omnium Doctorum.

And in a former passage (lib. ii., c. 9) he said, "The whole world was bound by the force of custom, and this alone was opposed to those who wished to introduce novelties." But in this place matters of this kind are not in question. That, however, which is added at the end of the Article is most true, and St. Augustine says the same (ep. 86, *ad Casulanum*, and ep. 119 ad *Januarium*); and again it is to be found, 31 dist. cap. *Quoniam*, &c., and cap. *Aliter*, and is the opinion of all the Doctors.

Articulus XXXV.—*De Homiliis.*

TOMUS secundus **Homiliarum,** quarum singulos titulos huic Articulo subjunximus, continet piam et salutarem doctrinam, et his temporibus necessariam, non minus quàm prior tomus Homiliarum; quæ editæ sunt tempore Edwardi VI. itaque eas in Ecclesiis per ministros diligenter et clare, ut à populo intelligi possint, recitandas esse judicavimus.*

Article XXXV.—*Of the Homilies.*

THE second Book of Homilies, the several titles whereof we have joined under this Article, doth contain a godly and wholesome Doctrine, and necessary for these times, as doth the former Book of Homilies, which were set forth in the time of *Edward* the Sixth; and therefore we judge them to be read in Churches by the Ministers, diligently and distinctly, that they may be understanded of the people.

Paraphrasis. — Multa quidem sunt in Homiliis laude digna, alia

Explanation.—There are many things in the Homilies worthy of all

---

* The List of the Titles of the Homilies is omitted in both editions of this treatise.

nec nobis, vel doctioribus eorum, arrident. Nec tenentur Protestantes, ob hæc verba in Articulo, statim in singula verba vel sententias Homiliarum jurare, nam ut olim Turrecremata, cum ipsa Ecclesia Doctorum aliquorum opuscula probat, non ob id intelligendum est, omnia in eis contenta probari: sicut in Constitutionibus sextæ Synodi, aliquorum Doctorum opera probata sunt, quod etiam in **Decretis legitur, dist. 15, non tamen omnia verba et** particulas approbat, **ut conveniunt Doctores.** Hoc etiam exactissimè tradunt Doctores Parisienses, exponentes Bullam Urbani quinti approbantem doctrinam S. Thomæ, in qua scripsit Tholosanis, *ejus doctrinam ut bene dictam, et Catholicam teneri debere. Dicunt tamen Parisienses, prædictam approbationem non esse universalem, sed tanquam doctrinæ utilis, et in multis probabilis,* prudenter igitur quæ sanam doctrinam sapiunt, populo legenda, alia neglectui habenda.

praise; other matters neither please us, nor the more learned among them. Nor are Protestants, because of these words in the Article, directly bound to hold every word or sentence in the Homilies; for, as was said long since by Turrecremata, when the Church herself approves the works of certain Doctors, it is not, therefore, to be understood that everything contained in those works is approved, as in the Constitutions of the Sixth Synod the works of certain Doctors were approved, as is read in the Decrees, dist. 15; but the Synod did not approve every word and clause, as the Doctors agree. This opinion, too, the Parisian Doctors most exactly set forth in explaining the Bull of Urban V., approving the doctrine of St. Thomas, in which he wrote to those of Toulouse, that "his doctrine ought to be well expressed and Catholic; but the Parisians say that the approbation aforesaid is not universal, but implies that the doctrine is useful, and in many things probable." Those things, therefore, which savour of sound doctrine, should prudently be read by the people, the rest should be neglected.

ARTICULUS XXXVI.—*De Episcoporum, et Ministrorum Consecratione.*

LIBELLUS de consecratione Archiepiscoporum, et Episcoporum, et ordinatione Presbyterorum, et Diaconorum editus nuper temporibus Edwardi VI. et authoritate Parliamenti illis ipsis temporibus confirmatus, omnia ad ejusmodi consecrationem et ordinationem necessaria continet: et nihil habet quod ex se sit aut superstitiosum, aut impium: itaque quicunque juxta ritus illius libri consecrati, aut ordinati sunt, ab anno secundo prædicti Regis Edwardi usque ad hoc tempus, aut in posterum juxta eosdem ritus consecrabuntur, aut ordinabuntur, rite atque ordinate* atque legitime statuimus esse et fore consecratos et ordinatos.

PARAPHRASIS.—Hic Articulus nos remittit ad Pontificale sub Edvardo VI. compactum.

De ordinatione Episcoporum verba in ceremoniali illo sunt: *Accipe Spiritum Sanctum, et memento suscitare gratiam Dei, quæ est in te per impositionem manuum, quia Deus non nobis dedit Spiritum timoris, sed potestatis et sobrietatis.*

ARTICLE XXXVI.—*Of Consecration of Bishops and Ministers.*

THE Book of Consecration of Archbishops and Bishops, and Ordering of Priests and Deacons, lately set forth in the time of *Edward* the Sixth, and confirmed at the same time by the authority of Parliament, doth contain all things necessary to such Consecration and Ordering: neither hath it any thing, that of itself is superstitious and ungodly. And therefore whosoever are consecrated or ordered according to the Rites of that Book, since the second year of the forenamed King *Edward* unto this time, or hereafter shall be consecrated or ordered according to the same Rites; we decree all such to be rightly, orderly, and lawfully consecrated and ordered.

EXPLANATION.—This Article refers us to the Pontifical compiled under Edward VI.

At the ordination of Bishops, the words in that ceremonial are: "Take the Holy Ghost, and remember that thou stir up the grace of God which is in thee by imposition of hands; for God hath not given us the spirit of fear, but of power and soberness."

---

* In some editions "ordine" for "ordinate."

Hæc verba simul cum impositione manuum à pluribus Episcopis facta, pronuntiat Archiepiscopus: quibus peractis tradit in manus consecrandi Biblia, cum verbis accommodatis: adeo ut forma sit, *Accipe Spiritum Sanctum*, etc. materia, impositio manuum, judicent doctiores an hanc eorum consecrationem ex hoc capite irritam defineri fas sit, præsertim, cum Vasq. et alii putent impositionem manuum, et illa verba sufficere quantum est de jure divino, ad essentiam ordinationis Episcopalis: ut videre est, p. 3, disp. 240, num. 58. Conink de Ordine, disp. 20, dub. 7, num. 58, fuse, et probat ex Trid.; nec dissentit Arcudius de Sacramento Ordinis, propter authoritatem Scripturæ, quæ horum duorum sæpius et solum mentionem facit, ubi etiam fuse ostendit in Ecclesia Græca traditiones instrumentorum non esse necessarias simpliciter, nec formas illis applicatas.

The Archbishop pronounces these words at the same time, with the imposition of hands by several Bishops, which being done, he gives into the hands of the person to be consecrated a Bible with suitable words: so that the form is, "Take the Holy Ghost," &c. The matter is the imposition of hands; let the more learned judge whether it be right to declare their consecration void on this account, especially since Vasquez and others think that the imposition of hands and those words are sufficient, *jure divino*, for the essence of the ordination of a Bishop, as may be seen from the writings of Vasquez, p. iii., disp. 240, num. 58. *Conink de Ord.*, disp. xx., dub. 7, num. 58, at length treats of the question, and proves it from the Council of Trent; nor does Arcudius dissent from this opinion (*de Sacr. Ord.*), because of the authority of Scripture, which makes mention of these two points alone, and most frequently. He also, in the same place, shows that in the Greek Church the delivery of the instruments is not necessary, absolutely, nor the forms connected with them.

Idem judicium facit de unctione physica et materiali in Sacramento Ordinis, sive quoad Episcopos vel sacerdotes; non enim est essentialis, secundum eum: immo in Ecclesia Græca nunquam fuit adhibita, ut contendit Arcudius; quia Chrys. in Digressione Morali 2, Orat. in 1, ad Timoth., faciens distinctionem inter sacerdotes veteris et novæ legis, dicit priores unctos fuisse. Dionys. etiam, licet accuratissimus in ceremoniis describendis, nec verbum habet de unctione, quando vero aliqui Græci Patres, de unctione mentionem faciunt, de spirituali eos intelligit.

De Presbyteris forma est, *Accipe Spiritum Sanctum, quorum remiseris peccata, remittuntur eis, et quorum retinueris retenta sunt, et esto fidelis verbi divini, et sanctorum Sacramentorum ejus dispensator, in Nomine Patris, etc.* Postea traduntur Evangelia, et dicit: *Accipe potestatem prædicandi Dei Verbum, sanctorumque Sacramentorum administrandi in hac congregatione.*

His judgment is the same respecting the physical and material unction in the Sacrament of Order, whether with respect to Bishops or Priests; for it is not essential, according to him: moreover, in the Greek Church, as Arcudius argues, it never has been used, because St. Chrysostom (*Digress. Mor. 2, Orat. in 1 ad Timoth.*), distinguishing between the priests of the Old and the New Law, says that the former were anointed. St. Dionysius, again, though most accurate in describing ceremonies, says not a word respecting unction; and when some Greek Fathers mention unction, he understands them to mean spiritual unction.

With respect to Priests the form is, "Receive the Holy Ghost; whose sins thou dost forgive they are forgiven; and whose sins thou dost retain they are retained. And be thou a faithful dispenser of the Word of God, and of His Holy Sacraments; in the Name of the Father," &c. Then the Gospels [Bible] are given into the candidate's hand, and the Bishop says: "Take thou authority to preach the Word of God, and to minister the Holy Sacraments in this congregation."

Christus quidem primo potestatem dedit super Corpus Christi verum, postea super mysticum, ut patet in sacro textu, et optime declarat Doctor 4, dist. 24, sic etiam practicat Ecclesia, ut patet in Pontificali. Aliqui Doct. tenent, ut q. 37, dub. 2, in supplementum D. Th. post Bell. notavit doctissimus Kellis. (cui multam tribuo, et ex multis titulis debeo) quod in ordinatione sacerdotum, illa secunda potestas super corpus mysticum, per potestatem remittendi et ligandi, solum sit explicativa seu declarativa potestatis ante traditæ, et non esse aliquam novam potestatem de novo collatam, sic aliqui Thomistæ, ut patet apud Capreol. 4, d. 19, quæst. 1, quod meliori jure alii putant dici in hac Nostratium forma, scilicet in prioribus verbis, solum explicari, quod posteà traditur, quia *super omnia Sacramenta*, potestas confertur in verbis sequentibus, ut directe ibi astruitur, ergo etiam super Sacramentum Pœnitentiæ, quod in prioribus verbis insinuabatur; ubi etiam intelligi non dubito, potestatem sacrificandi, quia datur potestas super Corpus Christi verum, de jure verò divino non fit consecratio nisi in Sacrificio, ut fere unanimis est con-

Christ, indeed, first gave power over the true Body of Christ, afterwards over His mystical Body, as is plain in Holy Writ; the Doctor well declares (4 dist., 24), and this is the practice of the Church, as is plain in the Pontifical. Some Doctors hold (as in qu. 37, dub. 2, sup.) St. Thomas, after Bellarmine, the very learned Kellison (whose debtor I am on many grounds) that in the Ordination of Priests, that second power over the mystical body, by the power of loosing and binding, is only explicative or declarative of the power given before, and is not any new power given afresh. So say some of the Thomists, as appears from Capreol. 4, d. 19, qu. 1, which others with more justice think is said of the form in use in this country, namely, that in the former words that is only explained which is subsequently given, because in the following words power is given *in all the Sacraments*, as is expressly added in that form, and therefore in the Sacrament of Penance, which was implied by the former words, where, too, I doubt not but that the power of offering sacrifice is understood, because power is given over Christ's true Body; but

sensus Doctorum, et Christus ipse dando potestatem consecrandi, dedit insimul sacrificandi, ut patet in ultima Cœna.

Scio Puritanos dicere, in hac eorum forma ex proposito expungi potestatem Sacrificandi ut superstitiosam. Sed non contra illos ago, quia vere destruunt totam formam: benigne solum expono Articulum, et eo plus quo video celebriores Protestantium Doctores, ut superius ostendi, Sacerdotes et Sacrificia agnoscere. Peccant saltem in omni sententia non observando formam ab Ecclesia Latina demandatam, ut cum Soto tenent Doctores; ut etiam videre est apud Petigianis in 4, de Baptismo, et Doctorem, 4, dist. 8, quia est *de necessitate Ministri*, ut loquitur Doctor, id est præcepti in Ecclesia Latina. Fusè etiam de hoc agit Doctor, d. 3, q. 2.

Sed an illa forma sufficiat ad Sa-

by divine right there is no **consecration** except in the Sacrifice, as is the almost unanimous consent of the Doctors; and Christ Himself, by giving the power of consecrating, gave at the same time that of sacrificing, as appears in the narrative of the Last Supper.

I know that the Puritans say that in this form of theirs the power of sacrificing is purposely expunged, as being superstitious. But I am not writing against them, because in truth they destroy the whole form. I merely explain the Article in a favourable sense, and the rather because I find that the more distinguished Doctors of the Protestants, as I have shown above, acknowledge Priests and a Sacrifice. At least they err according to every opinion by not observing the form commanded by the Latin Church, as Soto holds with the Doctors, as appears also from *Petigianis de Bapt.* 4, and from the Doctor, 4, dist. 8, because the form is *de necessitate Ministri*, as the Doctor says, that is, necessary by precept in the Latin Church. The Doctor treats on this at length, too, d. 3, qu. 2.

But the question is, Is that form

cerdotium. Videtur (non asserendo, minus adhærendo) responderi posse secundum aliquos, quod sic, ex Innocentius IV. in Cap. Presbyt. de Sacramentis non iterandis, ubi dicit: *De ritu Apostolico invenitur, quod manus imponebant ordinandis, et quod orationem fundebant super eos. Aliam autem formam non invenimus ab eis servatam. Unde credimus, quod nisi essent formæ posteà inventæ, sufficeret* **ordinatori dicere** *Sis Sacerdos, vel alia æquipollentia, sed subsequentibus temporibus formas, quæ servantur, Ecclesia ordinavit.* Ipsius ergo, et constans est **Doctorum** sententia, substantiam **formæ** in omni ordinatione, non esse præcisè in cortice verborum, sed sensu: modo igitur fiat verbis æquipollentibus, ut loquitur Innoc. non dubito sufficere et valere: *Non enim verba,* **sed rem opinor spectari oportere:** ut **Arcudius** ubi suprà. Et Trid. videtur favere, sess. 23, c. 4, ubi ait: *Sacram ordinationem verbis et signis exterioribus perfici.* Ubi non determinat verba vel signa. Multi utique Doctores non improbabiliter existimant, nec verba, nec symbola externa, id est, nec formam vel materiam à Christo determinate esse **assignata,** sed ab Ecclesia assig-

sufficient for conferring the Priesthood? It seems (I do not assert it, still less do I hold to the opinion) that, according to some, it might be answered affirmatively from Innocent IV. (*De Sacra non iter Cap. Presbyt.*), where it is said, "With regard to the Apostolic Ritual, we find that they used to impose hands on those who were to be ordained, and prayed over them. Nor do we find any other form observed by them. Whence we believe, that unless forms had been subsequently invented, it would suffice for the ordainer to say, Be thou a Priest, or equivalent words; but, in subsequent times, the Church ordained the forms which are now observed." It is, therefore, his opinion, and a constant one with the Doctors, that the substance of the form in all ordination, is not absolutely in the mere husk of the words, but in their sense; if only then it be done in equivalent words, as Innocent says, "I have no doubt but that it is sufficient and effectual. For I think that it is needful to look, not at the words, but at the matter;" as says Arcudius, *ubi supra,* and the Council of Trent seems to favour

nanda. Solum igitur Christo ordinatum est secundum hanc sententiam, quod ordinatio fiat aliquibus verbis et symbolis. Et hinc à fortiori sequitur, verba æquipollentia omnino sufficere, quia multo facilius, verba ab Ecclesia, quam si à Christo assignentur, modo in sensu et re conveniant, aliquantulum mutari possint. Unde Græci hac forma utuntur: *Divina gratia, quæ semper infirma sanat, et quæ decent supplet, creat seu promovet N. venerabilem Subdiaconum in Diaconum, venerabilem Diaconum in Presbyterum, Deo amabilissimum Presbyterum in Episcopum.* Ubi patet eos rite ordinari, quia substantiam habent. Idem plane aliis videtur, sine assertione esse judicium de forma Nostratium, quia potestatem sacrificandi et absolvendi involvunt, nisi alio detorquere malint, sicut Puritani fecerunt, et à Nostris optime excepti sunt.

the opinion, sess. 23, cap. 4, where it says that holy order " is performed [*perficitur*] by words and outward signs," where it does not specify the words or the signs. Many Doctors, too, not improbably think that neither words nor outward symbols, that is, neither the form nor matter, were determinately prescribed by Christ, but were to be prescribed by the Church. According to this opinion, therefore, Christ only appointed that ordination should be conferred with some form of words and symbols, and from this it follows *à fortiori*, that equivalent words are wholly sufficient, because words prescribed by the Church can much more readily be slightly changed than if they had been prescribed by Christ. So that the Greeks use this form: "The grace of God, which always strengthens things that are weak, and supplies what are fitting, makes or promotes N. venerable sub-deacon to be a deacon, venerable deacon to be a priest, priest most beloved by God to be a bishop." Where it is plain that they differ from the form of the Latins; no one, however, denies that they are rightly ordained, because

Quod si hoc durum videatur aliquibus nostrum, attendant ad illud Doctoris, 4, d. 8, q. 2, §. Ex hoc patet: *Est dictum minus discretum, asserere, quod necesse est in quolibet Sacramento scire præcisè, quæ verba sunt de forma, ad hoc, ut aliquis conferat Sacramentum. Istud enim manifestè falsum est, non solum in Eucharistia, sed etiam in Baptismo, et Pœnitentia et Sacramento Ordinis, forte enim nullus est qui sciat pro certo, nec Episcopus, nec Ordinatus, quæ sint præcise verba ordinationis in Sacerdotem: Et tamen non est dicendum, quod nullus est ordinatus in Sacerdotem in Ecclesia. Consimiliter diversi utuntur diversis verbis in conferendo Sacramentum Pœnitentiæ: nec est certum de aliquibus verbis præcisis, quæ sint illa, non tamen dicendum est, quod nullus absolvatur in Ecclesia.*

they have the substance. The same appears to others to be the right conclusion respecting the form used in this country, because it includes the power of sacrificing and absolving, unless men choose to twist the meaning another way, as the Puritans have done, and have been well censured by writers on our side.

But if this should seem hard to some on our side, let them consider the opinion of the Doctor, 4, d. 8, qu. 2, § *Ex hoc patet*. "It is an imprudent affirmation, to assert that it is necessary in every Sacrament to know precisely what words constitute the form, to the end that any one should confer the Sacrament. For that is manifestly false, not only in the Eucharist, but also in Baptism, Penance, and the Sacrament of Order. Possibly there is no one, whether Bishop or Candidate for Orders, who knows for certain, what are precisely the words of ordination for a Priest; and yet it must not be said that no one is ordained for a Priest in the Church. In like manner different persons use different words in conferring the Sacrament of Penance, nor is it certain respecting any precise words, which

Unde illustrissimus Scholiator dicit, licet certæ essent formæ in Sacramentis, tamen quælibet verba earum formarum non sunt adeo certa et determinata, quum alia sufficiant.

Quod autem additur in ceremoniali, quod Presbyteri præsentes etiam imponant manus in capita ordinandorum, fuit expresse ordinatum in 4, Carth. cap. 3, hoc tamen non observatur à Græcis, licet semper in Ecclesia Latina propter authoritatem Pauli ad Tim. 4. *Noli negligere gratiam quæ data est tibi cum impositione manuum Presbyterii.* Sic etiam loquitur Trid. sess. 14, can. 3, secus vero est in ordinatione Diaconi, ut habetur in Carthag. c. 4.

De Diaconis forma est: *Accipe potestatem, et officium Diaconi in Ecclesia Dei tibi commissa exercendi. In Nomine Patris,* etc. Posteà in traditione Bibliorum dicit: *Accipe potestatem legendi Evangelium in Eccle-*

they may be, yet it is not to be said that no one is absolved in the Church.

Whence the celebrated Schoolman says, Though there be fixed forms in the Sacraments, nevertheless all the words of those forms are not so fixed and determined, since others may suffice.

The part which is added in the Ceremonial, that the Priests who are present also lay their hands on the heads of those who are to be ordained, was expressly ordered by the fourth Council of Carthage, cap. 3; this however, is not observed by the Greeks, though it always is in the Latin Church on the authority of St. Paul, 1 Tim. 4: "Neglect not the gift which was given thee by prophecy, with the laying on of the hands of the presbytery." So too speaks the Council of Trent, sess. 14, can. 3; in the ordination of a Deacon however, the rule is different, *Conc. Carth.* c. 4.

In ordaining Deacons the form is "Take thou authority to execute the office of a Deacon in the Church of God committed unto thee. In the name of the Father, &c." Then in giving to each of them the Sacred

sia Dei, et idem prædicandi, si ad illud præstandum ordinarie vocatus fueris.

Multis videtur nullum essentiale hic prætermitti, secundum declarationem Florentini vel Trident. propter rationes superius assignatas. Impositio manuum omnium fere consensu est essentialis, quæ hic recte observatur, quia simul cum probatione formæ tradunt etiam hic Evangelium, quod aliqui Theologi putant essentiale: sed ut recte Arcudius de Sacramento Ordinis (qui melius omnibus aliis hæc ad fundum examinavit) traditio instrumentorum est potius determinatio materiæ quàm ipsa materia, et sic intelligi debet Florent. secundum eum, quando specificat traditionem materiæ ad singulos ordines.

Addam hic opportunè pulcherrimum dictum Doctoris 4, d. 8, qu. 2, §. *Quod ergo erit consilium: Non est tutum alicui se reputare valde peritum de scientia sua, et dicere, volo uti præcisè istis verbis pro consecra-*

Books the officiant says, "Take thou authority to read the Gospel in the Church of God, and to preach the same, if thou be thereunto ordinarily commanded."

To many it seems that nothing essential is here omitted, according to the declaration either of Florence or of Trent, for the reasons assigned before. The imposition of hands is essential, by the consent of nearly all writers, which is in this office duly observed, for together with the pronouncing the form the Gospels too are given in this rite, which some theologians consider essential, but as Arcudius rightly observes, *de Sacr. Ordinis* (who has examined this matter to the bottom better than all others), the delivery of the instruments is rather the determination of the matter than the matter itself, and the Council of Florence should be understood in this sense, according to him, when it specifies the delivery of the matter for each order.

I will add here a beautiful saying of the Doctor's, much to the point, 4, d. 8, qu. 2, § *Quod ergo erit consilium:* "It is not safe for anyone to esteem himself highly skilled on account of his knowledge, and to say,

tione, sed securior est simplicitas, volo ista verba proferre sub ea intentione, sub qua Christus instituit ea esse proferenda, et quæ ex Christi institutione sunt de forma, dico ut de forma, et quæ ad reverentiam, ad reverentiam. Hæc ille: utinam conditores **Articulorum** eadem qua Doctor **humilitate Sacramentorum formas pro rei gravitate perpendissent, non adeo facilè formas in Ecclesia usitatas** *experitiæ suæ nimia reputatione;* ullo modo immutassent, vel detruncassent, licet forte (secundum opiniones toleratas) **non substantialiter.**

Ergo alia capita non examino de successione Episcoporum vel Ministrorum (ab aliis fusè et doctè peractum est) sed solum ipsa verba Articuli, an scilicet in formæ et materiæ (si nihil aliud obstat) valide fiat Ordinatio.

I choose to use precisely such and such words for the consecration; **but it is more secure to say simply, I wish to utter such and such words with that intention, with which** Christ appointed that they should be uttered; and those things which by Christ's institution are essential to the form, I say as essential to the form, and what is instituted for the sake of reverence, I say for the sake of reverence." Such are his words: would that the framers of the Articles had considered, with the same humility as the Doctor, the forms of the Sacraments as the gravity of the matter deserves, they would not then so easily, *from too great opinion of their own skill,* in any way, though it may be (according to opinions which are tolerated) not substantially, have changed or mutilated the forms used in the Church.

I do not then examine the other points respecting the succession of Bishops or Ministers (it has been treated at length and skilfully by others), but only the bare words of the Article, whether that is, in point of form and matter (if nothing else hinder), the Ordination be validly performed.

Articulus XXXVII.—*De Civilibus Magistratibus.*

REGIA Majestas in hoc Angliæ Regno ac cæteris ejus Dominiis summam habet potestatem ad quam omnium statuum hujus Regni, sive illi Ecclesiastici sint, sive civiles, in omnibus causis suprema gubernatio pertinet, et nulli externæ jurisdictioni est subjecta, nec esse debet.

Cum Regiæ Majestati summam gubernationem tribuimus, quibus titulis intelligimus animos quorundam calumniatorum offendi, non damus Regibus nostris, aut verbi Dei, aut Sacramentorum administrationem, quod etiam injunctiones ab Elizabetha Regina nostra nuper editæ, apertissime testantur, sed eam tantum prærogativam quam in sacris Scripturis à Deo Ipso, omnibus piis principibus videmus semper fuisse attributam: hoc est, ut omnes status atque ordines fidei suæ a Deo commissos, sive illi Ecclesiastici sint, sive civiles in officio contineant, et contumaces ac delinquentes gladio civili coërceant.

Romanus Pontifex nullam habet jurisdictionem in hoc regno Angliæ.

Leges regni possunt Christianos propter capitalia et gravia crimina morte punire.

Article XXXVII.—*Of the Civil Magistrates.*

THE King's Majesty hath the chief power in this Realm of *England*, and other his Dominions, unto whom the chief Government of all Estates of this Realm, whether they be Ecclesiastical or Civil, in all causes doth appertain, and is not, nor ought to be, subject to any foreign Jurisdiction.

Where we attribute to the King's Majesty the chief government, by which Titles we understand the minds of some slanderous folks to be offended; we give not to our Princes the ministering either of God's Word, or of the Sacraments, the which things the Injunctions also lately set forth by *Elizabeth* our Queen do most plainly testify; but that only prerogative, which we see to have been given always to all godly Princes in Holy Scriptures by God Himself; that is, that they should rule all states and degrees committed to their charge by God, whether they be Ecclesiastical or Temporal, and restrain with the civil sword the stubborn and evildoers.

The Bishop of *Rome* hath no jurisdiction in this Realm of *England*.

The Laws of the Realm may punish Christian men with death, for heinous and grievous offences.

Christianis licet ex mandato Magistratus arma portare, et justa bella administrare.

PARAPHRASIS. — Hic Articulus subministrat materiam examinandi quæstionem longe gravissimam. An scilicet, laici sint capaces jurisdictionis spiritualis.

Primo advertendum ex omnium sententia illos non esse capaces clavium, quia tunc etiam remissionis seu absolutionis à peccatis.

Secundo advertendum, jurisdictionem spiritualem, seu potestatem jurisdictionis, non esse immediate ipsam potestatem clavium, immo separabiles, nec actu semper conjungi, vel jure divino, vel positivo.

Tertio supponendum, Summum Pontificem in omni sententia, secundum absolutam potentiam suam, posse jurisdictionem talem laïcis concedere, quia non expresse contra jus divinum, ut recte Soto 4, dist. 20, quæst. 1, art. 4, sic etiam Miranda in Manuali quæst. 3, art. 2, et hoc non solum respectu virorum, sed fœminarum. Addit tamen Miranda hoc respectu fœminarum nusquam adhuc

It is lawful for Christian men, at the commandment of the Magistrate, to wear weapons, and serve in the wars.

EXPLANATION.—This Article affords by far the most weighty subject of examination; whether, that is, laics are capable of exercising spiritual jurisdiction.

First, it must be observed, that by consent of all they are not capable of exercising the power of the keys, for then they would be able to confer absolution or remission of sins.

Secondly, it must be observed, that spiritual jurisdiction, or the power of jurisdiction, is not directly the power of the keys itself; indeed that they are separable, and are not always actually united, either by divine or positive law.

Thirdly, it must be supposed, that the Sovereign Pontiff in every matter, in virtue of his absolute power, can confer such jurisdiction on laics, because it is not directly against divine law, as is rightly observed by Soto (4, dist. 20, qu. 1, art. 4) and likewise Miranda (*Manual*, qu. 3, art. 2); and this not only in respect of men but also of women. Miranda, however, adds

concessum, quod tamen negat D. **Aluin. c. 3,** de Episcopis, Abbatibus et Abbatissis c. 22, et citat multa **jura, ex quibus actu** conceditur Abbatissis potestas jurisdictionis, non quidem excommunicandi per se, sed præcipiendi suis subditis Sacerdotibus, ut excommunicent rebelles et contumaces moniales; et hoc valere vel ex jure communi, vel consuetudine, vel saltem ex privilegio, vel strictius loquendo, dicendum cum Laimanno lib. i. tract. 5, **p.** 1, cap. 3, num. 3 et 4, quod non habent jurisdictionem **spiritualem proprie, sed** *usuram quandam* **jurisdictionis. Et** hinc conferre possunt beneficia, et instituere **clericos** in Ecclesiis ad Monasterium suum pertinentibus, etc.

Ut sensum meum in re tam gravi aperiam, dicendum putem, nullo quidem jure, ut prætactum est, eis competere potestatem seu jus spirituale, ut loquitur Joannes de Parisiis De Potestate Papæ, c. 21, quo gratia spiritualis causatur, id **est**, potestas administrandi Sacramenta. Et idem est judicium de potestate quæ consequitur ex priori, ut est

that this has no where yet been conceded in respect of women; which, **however,** is denied by D. Aluin (c. 3, ***De Episcopis Abbatibus et*** *Abbatissis*, c. 22), who cites many decrees by which the power of **jurisdiction is** conceded to Abbesses, not indeed the power of excommunication itself, but the power of commanding priests under their jurisdiction to excommunicate rebellious and contumacious nuns; and that this is of force either **by** common law, or by custom, or at least by privilege; but to speak more exactly, we must say with Layman (lib. 1, tract. 5, p. 1, cap. 3, num. 3 and 4), that they have not spiritual jurisdiction properly, but a certain use of jurisdiction. And by this **they are** able to confer benefices, and **to institute clerks** to churches belonging to their monasteries, &c.

But to shew my own opinion in a matter of such gravity, I think it should be said, that by no right, as has been said before, **are they** capable of spiritual power **or** jurisdiction (as says John of Paris, *De Potestate Papæ*, c. 21), whereby spiritual grace is procured, that is to **say,** the power of administering the Sacraments. And my opinion is the

inflictio pœnæ **spiritualis, scripturarum** expositio, ministrorum Ecclesiæ institutio, confirmatio, vel examen, et alia id genus multa. Quodvis enim horum de jure divino restringitur præcise ad homines spirituales seu Deo sacros, ut olim definitum est a Joan. xxii. contra Marsilium de Padua, ut videre est apud Turrecrem. l. 4. Summæ, sub finem.

Cæterum quoad potestatem seu jus antecedens non de per se et necessário annexum spiritualibus officiis, bene potest in laïcis subinde residere; sicut præsentatio, collatio beneficiorum, punitio temporalis clericorum, et alia id genus multa, ut dixi de Abbatissis, præcipue ex concessione Ecclesiæ, vel longa consuetudine præscripta, conniventibus prælatis Ecclesiæ.

Dixi et merito, etiam ex consuetudine, quia non solum concessio, sed consuetudo ipsa tribuit jurisdictionem etiam in spiritualibus, ut docet Innocent. in cap. Novit. de **judic.** et multi præsertim, quando

same respecting the power which flows from the former, such as the infliction of spiritual penalties, the exposition of the Scriptures, the **institution, confirmation, or examination** of the ministers of the Church, and many things of that kind. For **everything of this kind is by divine law absolutely restricted to spiritual** men, or consecrated to God, as was long ago defined by John xxii. against Marsilius of Padua, as may be seen in Turrecremata (l. 4, *Summæ*, *sub finem*).

But as respects the power, or antecedent right, not of itself and necessarily annexed to spiritual offices, **this may** occasionally rest with laics, **such as the presentation or collation** of benefices, **the temporal punishment** of clerks, and many other **things of that kind,** as I said concerning Abbesses, principally by concession of the Church, or sanctioned by long custom, the prelates of the Church assenting to it.

And I said with **good reason,** sanctioned by long custom, because not only concession but custom itself gives jurisdiction, even in spiritual matters, as Innocent teaches (cap. *Novit. de judic.*), and many others,

consuetudinis exercitium à tempore immemoriali probatur, ut declarant Juristæ, de qua re vide Salgado p. i. c. 1. Prælud. 3, n. 122, et deinceps.

Dices hic non solum concedi Principibus nostris potestatem ex consuetudine, seu concessione, sed supremam; ut ibi asseritur, quod non potest eis competere in spiritualibus, ut omnes Doctores tenent.

Respondeo, quod Doctores prædicti asserant Papam non posse auferre jurisdictionem Principum ex consuetudine vel concessione firma, valide et licite introductam: sicut satis insinuat Navar. c. 27, in Enchir. n. 70, agens de Gallis. Sic etiam Salzedo in Scholiis ad praxim criminalem Bernardi Diaz. c. 55, § Apud Gallos, qui hinc putat Bullam Cœnæ non intelligi contra privilegia remuneratoria, vel quæ sunt firmata consuetudine immemoriali, prout etiam Nav. Tandem Duvallius de dis. Eccles. p. 3, fol. 405, dicit, quod Papa quando dat privilegium Principibus secularibus in materia jurisdictionis humano jure (id est, non contra jus divinum), introductæ, non

especially when the exercise of the custom is proved to have been from time immemorial, as the Jurists say, on which point see Salgado, p. 1, c. 1, *Prælud.* 3, n. 122, &c.

You will say that not only is this power derived from custom or from concession granted to our princes, but even the supreme power, as is asserted in the Article, of which they are not capable in spiritual matters, as all the Doctors hold.

I reply that the Doctors just mentioned assert that the Pope cannot take away the jurisdiction of princes derived from established custom or concession, validly and lawfully introduced: as Navar implies (*Enchir.* n. 70, c. 27), treating of the French. And so too Salzedo in his Scholia on the Crim. prax. of Bernard Diaz. (c. 55, § *Apud Gallos*), who from this considers that the Bull *Cœnæ* is not to be understood against the remunerative privileges, or those which are confirmed by immemorial custom, as Navar says too. Lastly, Duval (*de Disc. Eccl.* p. 3, fol. 405) says that the Pope when he grants to secular princes privileges in matters of jurisdiction introduced by human

potest revocare, si concessum sit per modum *contractus vel concordati vel transitionis*. Et sine dubio sufficit ad intentum hujus Articuli, quod ideo dicatur, *suprema* potestas, non simpliciter, sed quia non per superiorem auferibilis. Regibus autem nostris fuisse sic concessum jus nominandi et providendi de beneficiis, testatur post alios Harpsf. sæculo 14, fuisse etiam aliam consuetudinem immemorialem ex privilegio ortam, causas clericorum cognoscendi patet ex decis. Rotæ. 804, ut communiter citatur. Quod si dixeris non constare de hoc privilegio, ut etiam Suarez lib. 4, de immunitate Eccles. c. 34, num. 12, responderent quod consuetudo notoria, licet non constiterit, est melius, quia in hoc casu magis operatur tacitum seu præsumptum privilegium, quia supponit concessionem irrevocabilem, secus si constaret de privilegio, quia non reciperet interpretationem, sed observandum erat, prout sonat, et plus operatur in hoc, fama privilegii cum immemoriali consuetudine, ut in terminis tradit Fulvius Pacian, Cons. fi. num. 124, ne propter difficultatem probandi rem antiquam, pereat jus partis: sic Camillus Borell. de Præ-

law, (that is, not against the divine law,) cannot revoke the grant, if it be made by way of *contract, or of concordat, or of transition*. And without any doubt this is sufficient for the intention of this Article, because it is called the chief (supreme) power, not, that is, in an absolute sense, but because it cannot be taken away by any superior. But that the right of nominating and providing for benefices was thus granted to our kings Harpsfield (*Sæc.* xiv.) testifies, together with others; and that there was another immemorial custom arising from privilege, of investigating the causes of clerks, is clear from the decision of the *Rotæ*, 804, as it is commonly quoted. But if you should say that this privilege was not granted by all, as Suarez (lib. 4, *de Immunit. Eccles.* c. 34, num. 12), they would reply that a notorious custom, though not granted by all, is better, because in this case a tacit or presumable privilege has more weight, because it presupposes an irrevocable concession; and the matter would be different were it a privilege, of which all granted the existence, for then it would not admit of any explanation, but would

stantia Regis Catholici, c. 503, n. 26 et 27.

Dices non solum in Articulo competere hanc potestatem Principibus nostris ex privilegio vel consuetudine, sed jure divino.

Respondeo, quod valde multi Doctores de hoc consulti, tenent, quod *Quoad commune bonum Reipubl.* principes habent jurisdictionem etiam in multis causis foro Ecclesiastico alias per se subjiciendis. Et hoc non solum *de jure divino positivo, sed naturali.* Sed rectiùs Doctores in Bullam Cœnæ, negant principibus jurisdictionem in clericos et eorum causas ex jure Regio, sed nudam potestatem civilem et temporalem, ob protectionem et defensionem Reipublicæ, justitiæ et pacis communis; et hoc de jure divino et naturali ipsis competit, nec hic Articulus plus exigit: et ratio quam tetigit Suarez

have had to be observed, according to the very letter; and in this matter the tradition of a privilege with immemorial custom has more weight, as is stated expressly by Fulvius Pacian (*Cons. fi.* num. 124), lest on account of the difficulty of proving an ancient matter the rights of any party should be lost: this is supported too by Camillus Borel (*de Præstantia Regis Cathol.* c. 503, n. 26 and 27).

You will say that, according to the Article, this power belongs to our princes not only by privilege or custom, but by divine law.

I reply that very many Doctors, being consulted on this point, hold that, *as far as the common good of the state is concerned,* princes have jurisdiction even in many causes otherwise in themselves subject to the ecclesiastical tribunal. And this *by divine law, not only positive but natural.* But Doctors, treating of the Bull *Cœnæ,* more rightly deny to princes jurisdiction over clerics and their causes by royal prerogative, beyond a bare civil and temporal authority, for the protection and defence of the state of justice and of the public peace; and this by divine and natural law belongs to them, nor

lib. 3, de Primatu Summi Pontificis c. 1, num. 4, in fine optime hanc partem probat. Quia humana natura non potest esse destitua remediis ad suam conservationem necessariis: accedit etiam Morl. in Empor. jur. 1, p. tit. 2, de legibus num. 20, vers. *Quia cum Regnum*, ubi dicit, quod cui conceditur **regnum necessario** omnia censentur concessa, sine quibus Regnum gubernari non potest: Regnum vero gubernari non posset nisi Principes hoc potestate poterentur, etiam in clericos, etc., ergo. Sic illi.

In hunc igitur finem, et in hoc sensu, magna sine dubio est potestas Regum jure divino et naturali secundum illos, in personas et causas **Ecclesiasticas in multis casibus** per accidens et indirectè, ut loquuntur Doctores; secundum partem directivam, seu imperativam; verbi gratiâ, **possunt civiliter mandare Clericis** etiam Episcopis, ut spiritualia sua ad pacem Reipublicæ disponant, ut dyscolos ex officiis amoveant, immo

does this Article require more; and the line of argument which Suarez has used (lib. 3, *de Summo Ponti.* c. 1, **num.** 4) towards the end most fully proves this portion, because human nature cannot be destitute of remedies necessary for its own preservation. To this may be added the authority of Morl (*in Empor. jur.* 1, p. tit. 2, *de Legibus*, num. 20, vers. *Quia cum Regnum*), where he says that to whom a kingdom is given of necessity are supposed to be given all those things without which the kingdom could not be governed. But the kingdom could not be governed unless princes had this power even over clerks, &c. Whence it follows, &c. Such are their arguments.

For this end, therefore, and in this sense, without doubt the kingly power is great both by divine and natural law, according to them, over ecclesiastical persons and causes in many cases, as the Doctors say, accidentally and indirectly, as respects the directing or commanding part; for instance, they can in a civil manner order clerks, who are even Bishops, to dispose their spiritual matters so as to conduce to the

innocentes Clericos ab injustis oppressionibus judicium. Ecclesiasticorum authoritate Regia defendere possunt. Et alia hujusmodi. Totum hoc confirmatur a Parsonio in Richardo II., Henrico IV., et Edwardo IV. et miratur, si aliquis negaret Regibus in suis regnis. Hic vide modestiam Navarri in Manuali, cap. 27, num. 69, ubi non dubitat de hoc dicto, modo sint veræ oppressiones et violentiæ. Vide etiam nu. 27.

Nec quoad substantiam rei multam discrepat Cajetanus, ubi inferius, nec Victor De Potestate Ecclesiastica. Et ratio convincit : nam clerici omnes, non obstante clericatu, sunt cives Reipublicæ et subditi Regis ratione domicilii, et consequenter ad leges Principum quatenus pertinent ad communem vivendi in Regno societatem, et ad justitiam exequendam quæ maxime pacem et tranquillitatem fovet, non possunt non astringi, nec ab illorum obedientia, vel in personis, vel causis prædictis, modo explicato eximi possunt, quantum ad pacem

peace of the state, and may remove the stubborn from their offices; moreover, by the kingly power they can protect innocent clerks from the unjust oppression of the ecclesiastical judges, and other matters of this kind. All this is confirmed by Parsons as respects Richard II., Henry IV., and Edward IV., and he expresses his surprise that any one should deny this power to kings within their realms. Remark here the moderation of Navar (*Manual*, cap. 27, num. 69), where he expresses no doubt as to this opinion, if only the oppression and violence be undoubted. See too num. 27.

Nor as respects the substance of the matter does Cajetan disagree with this (*see below*) nor Victor (*De Potestate Ecclesiastica*). And reason itself proves the same, for all clerks, notwithstanding their orders, are citizens of the state, and subjects of the king by reason of their domicile; and consequently they cannot escape being bound by the laws of princes (so far as they refer to the public manner of living in the kingdom), and to the acting with that justice which chiefly preserves peace and tranquillity; nor can they be exempted from the obe-

Reipublicæ necessarium est : nec putem ullum Doctorem Cathol. huic refragari. Unde Cajet. dicit Apol. de potestate Papæ cap. 27, quod *Principibus competat illa tyrannidi resistendi potestas, quam jure naturali et gentium habent, etiam in rebus Ecclesiasticis.* Et in hoc sensu ubivis terrarum Reges Christianissimi et Catholici hodie factitant; ut fusissime ostendere possum; nec plus hic asseritur. Præsertim si attendamus ad expositiones eorum in hunc Articulum; nullam utique jurisdictionem spiritualem Regibus nostris concedunt, sed gubernium civile et temporale indirecte et per accidens ob pacem Reipubl. in personas et causas prædictas Ecclesiasticas extensum. Sic D. Raynoldus licet Puritanus, D. Montacutius contra Heigham. et alii eorum doctissimi, quibuscum de hoc egi. Gavisus sum etiam valde de illo quod his diebus factum est Cantabrigiæ, in Comitiis pro actu doctorali, ab summo Pontifici, ut *Maximo Patri* (sic enim cum appellitabant), designata est cura spiritualium, Regi temporalium, licet sub finem subjiciebatur, Regum esse omnes *regere.* Quod intelligi debet civiliter, non spiritualiter, modo à nobis explicato.

dience due to them either in their persons, or in the causes above-mentioned in the manner which has been explained, as far as is necessary for the peace of the state; nor do I think that any Catholic Doctor is opposed to this opinion. Cajetan says (*Apol. de Potest. Papæ*, cap. 27) that "there pertains to princes that power of resisting tyranny which they have by natural law and the law of nations, even in ecclesiastical matters." And in this sense the Most Christian and Catholic kings are accustomed to act all over the world, as I could show at very great length, and no more is asserted by this Article. But especially if we consider the explanations of Anglicans on this Article, we shall see that they grant no spiritual jurisdiction whatever to our kings, but the civil and temporal government, indirectly and accidentally, for the peace of the state, extended over the above-mentioned ecclesiastical persons and causes. So says Dr. Reynolds, though a Puritan, Dr. Montagu against Heigham, and others of their most learned men with whom I have discoursed on this point. I was also extremely delighted at what was

Tandem ut summatim dicam, putem abunde sufficere huic Articulo, quod hodie à Gallis et Parliamento Parisiensi salva communione Ecclesiæ usurpatur.

Non ago partes eorum qui summa violentia trahi volunt hunc Articulum in defensionem jurisdictionis puræ spiritualis in Regibus, quod certissime hæreticum est.

Hæc liberius dixi, quia ut optime Cano l. 5, qu. 5 §. Nunc illud breviter: *Qui Summi Pontificis omne de re quacumque, judicium temere ac sine delectu defendant, eos sedis Apostolicæ authoritatem labefactare, non fovere, non firmare. Quid enim*

done lately at Cambridge, in the exercises for the Doctor's degree, where the care of spiritual matters was assigned to the Sovereign Pontiff as the *Chief Father* (for so they repeatedly called him), the care of temporals to the king, though at the end there was added that it was the office of kings to *rule* all persons, which ought to be understood civilly, not spiritually, in the manner explained by us.

Lastly, to sum all up, I think that the practice of the French and the Parliament of Paris at the present day, without prejudice to the communion of the Church, is fully enough to satisfy the meaning of this Article.

I will not act the part of those who, with the greatest violence, wish this Article to be forced into the defence of a purely spiritual jurisdiction in kings, which is certainly heretical.

I have said these things with less hesitation, because of what Canus has so well said (l. 5, qu. 5, § *Nunc illud breviter*): "They who rashly and without discrimination defend every decision on every matter of the Sovereign Pontiff, undermine

tandem adversum hæreticos disputando ille proficiet, quem viderint non judicio sed affectu patrocinium authoritatis Pontificiæ suscipere, nec id agere, ut disputationis suæ vi, lucem ac veritatem eliciat, sed ut se ad alterius sensum voluntatemque convertat? non eget Petrus mendacio nostro, nostra adulatione non eget. Hæc ille. Ego ingenuè dico, libentissime, ne dicam avidissime, ob justam defensionem Sedis Apostolicæ (divina gratia assistente) mortem subirem: *non enim animam meam me pretiosiorem facio.* Nec tamen quod justum est Principibus denegandum. Eousque solum processi.

Paragraphus sequens majori indiget glossa.

Forte tangit illam pervetustam quæstionem,—An Anglia sit feudatoria Papæ. Joannes, Rex Angliæ, ut testantur Matthæus Paris et Matthæus Westmonast. *de regione libera per chartam lugubrem ancil-*

the authority of the Apostolic See rather than strengthen or confirm it. For what possible end will he accomplish in disputing with heretics, whom they shall discover to take shelter under the authority of the Pontiff not from deliberation but from fancy, and to endeavour not by means of his arguments to elicit the truth, but **to accommodate himself to the opinions and wishes of his opponent?** Peter does **not require our subterfuges, nor our adulation.**" Such are his words. I will say openly, that most willingly, not to say with the greatest eagerness (by the assistance of God's grace), would I undergo death in **the just defence of the Apostolic See;** *for I do not esteem my life of more value than myself;* but at the same time we must not deny that which **is justly** due to princes. And so far only have I gone.

The next paragraph requires a wider explanation.

Perhaps it touches upon that very ancient question, whether England be a fief of the Pope. John, King of England, as is testified by Matthew Paris and Matthew of Westminster, "by a writing made of a

lam fecit et feudatariam Summo Pontifici. Henricus tamen ejus filius in Concil. Lugd. huic reclamavit, et præcipuè Episcopus Cant. ut testatur Walsing. ad annum 1245, et posteà Cancellarius Angliæ Episcopus Eliensis in publicis Regni Comitiis, consentientibus tribus Ordinibus Patriæ, reclamavit, non obstante privata sponsione Joannis, ut testatur Harps. ad sæc. 14, c. 5, immo et armis se à temporali jurisdictione Papæ defensuros protestabantur, sed quia hic inanis titulus S. Pontif. (ut cum reputabat olim illust. Tho. Morus, et hodie omnes Catholici), sæpius obtrudebatur ut aliqui dicunt, præsertim in principio Elizabethæ, à Paulo 4, quæ occupabat regnum, non requisito consensu Papæ, huic forte hic Articulus conditus est. *Multum enim inter fortunam privatam Principis, et Regale culmen interest,* ut Zeno l. ult. cap. de quadr. præscript.

free country a pitiable slave and vassal of the Sovereign Pontiff." His son Henry, however, at the Council of Lyons, protested against this, and so especially did the Bishop of Canterbury, as is testified by Walsingham, *ad ann.* 1245; and subsequently the Bishop of Ely, Chancellor of England, in the public Council of the kingdom, with the agreement of the three Estates of the Realm,* protested against it, notwithstanding the private agreement of John, as is narrated by Harpsfield (*ad Sæc.* 14, c. 5); and further, they declared that they would defend themselves by arms against the temporal jurisdiction of the Pope; and because this empty title of the Sovereign Pontiff (as it was esteemed by Sir Thomas More long since, and is now by all Catholics), was often put forward, as some say, particularly by Paul IV., at the commencement of the reign of Elizabeth, who took possession of the throne without obtaining the consent of the Pope,— therefore perhaps this Article was

---

* [The three Estates of the Realm, it may be remarked, were the Clergy, the Lords, and the Commons; **not**, as is commonly supposed at the present day, King, Lords, and Commons.]

Vel si hæc glossa minus placeat, tunc potest dici, adhuc hæc verba multiplicem ferre sensum; unus, quod omnimoda negatur subjectio et communio cum Sede Apostolica, quod est plane derelinquere Augustinum, Ambrosium, Hieronymum, etiam Cypr. Tertul. Irenæum et alios Ecclesiæ Christi splendores, qui ubique testantur se cum hac Sancta Sede communionem habuisse et subjectionem agnovisse.

De Ambrosio patet in cap. 3, 1 ad Tim. ubi vocat Damasum *Rectorem* totius Ecclesiæ, ergo et ipsius.

De Hieron. in Epist. ad Damasum, *Cathedræ Petri communione consocior.* Quid clarius? pulchra ibi habet ad eundem sensum.

De August. ep. 157, ad Optatum, fatetur se cum reliquis Episcopis ex Zosimi Papæ *mandato* Cæsariam

compiled. "For there is a great difference between the private estate of princes and the summit of the kingly power." Zeno, l. ult. cap. *de quad. Præscript.*

Or, if this explanation does not seem satisfactory, it may be said, that these words are capable of various meanings; one, that every kind of subjection and communion with the Apostolic See is denied, which is plainly to forsake Augustine, Ambrose, Jerome, together with Irenæus, Tertullian, Cyprian, and other bright lights of the Church of Christ, who everywhere testify that they had Communion with this Holy See, and acknowledged their subjection to it.

Of St. Ambrose this is plain, on 1 Tim. 3, where he calls Damasus "Ruler" of the whole Church, and therefore of himself.

Of St. Jerome, in his Epistle to Damasus: "I am associated in the communion of the Chair of Peter." What can be clearer? The same idea is beautifully expressed in those words.

Of St. Augustine (in *Ep.* 157, *Ad Optatum*), he states that he with other bishops had come to Cæsarea at the

venisse, etc. Altius potuissem conscendere et Cyprianum interpellare, qui Epist. 52, dicit communicare cum Pontifice Romano idem esse ac communicare cum Ecclesia Catholica.

Tertul. l. præscript. c. 36, *Habes Romam, unde nobis quoque authoritas est.* Ecce se subdidit authoritati Romani Pontificis testatur.

Irenæus utroque antiquior, l. 3, c. 3. *Ad hanc Ecclesiam, propter potentiorem principalitatem, necesse est omnem convenire Ecclesiam.* Res notoria **est, omnes** quotquot sancti fuerunt cum hac Sancta Sede communionem habuisse.

Alius sensus potest esse, quod insinuetur substractio ab obedientia, non Sedis Apostolicæ, seu authoritatis illi sedi annexæ, quantum est ad actum primum seu signatum, sed solum quantum ad actum exercitum (liceat parum extendere hos terminos Scholarum) id est, in quantum exerectur à tali persona, cui pro tempore commissa est Sedes illa.

command of Pope Zosimus, &c. I could go yet higher and introduce St. Cyprian, who (*Ep.* 52) says that **to communicate with the** Roman **Pontiff is the same thing as to** communicate with **the Catholic Church.**

Tertullian (*de Præscript. c.* **36**) : "You have Rome, whence too authority comes to us." He plainly testifies that he is subject to the authority of the Roman Pontiff.

St. Irenæus, who is more ancient than either of the others (*lib.* 3, *cap.* 3) : "With this Church, because of its greater authority, it is necessary that every Church should agree." **It is notorious** that all the Saints **who have ever existed have been in Communion with this Holy See.**

There may be another meaning, that there is implied a departure from the obedience—not of the Apostolic See, or **of** the authority annexed to that See as respects the act primarily, but only as respects the act when exercised (we may be **allowed** slightly to extend the meaning of these terms of the Schools), that is, as respects the **exercise of** that authority by such a person, to whom for a time that See is entrusted.

Primus sensus est quæstio juris, an scil. Sedi illi competat jurisdictio, seu dicendi jus in totam Ecclesiam, saltem secundum formam à Canonibus præscriptam (quod addo propter aliquos recentiores), et vere hoc Sanctæ Sedi negare, est plane contra sensum utriusque Ecclesiæ, nec de hoc uspiam fuit disceptatio in ullo Concilio, si recte ponderetur; Catholici etiam quotquot sunt vel fuerunt, huic subscripserunt; et satis evincitur ex ipso Nilo in fine, licet maximus sit adversarius Sedis Apostolicæ. Nec hoc dicit Articulus.

Secundus sensus videtur reduci posse ad duas quæstiones, unam etiam juris, alteram mixtam, scilicet tam juris, quam facti. Prima an hic et nunc liceat Regno alicui se subtrahere ab obedientia alicujus Pontificis ad tempus: de qua re scio quid resolvat Gerson, quæstione: *Quomodo et an liceat in causis fidei à summo Pontifice appellare, et ejus judicium declinare?* (cui multum in-

The first meaning is a question of right, whether, that is, to that See belongs jurisdiction, or the power of promulgating law through the whole Church, at least according to the form prescribed by the Canons; (this I add in consequence of some modern writers), and in truth to deny this to the Holy See is plainly contrary to the opinion of both the Eastern and Western Churches, nor was there ever any discussion respecting this point in any Council, if it be rightly considered. All Catholics too both of the present and past time, have agreed upon this, and it is clearly proved from Nilus towards the latter part, though he is a chief opponent of the Apostolic See. Nor does the Article make the above statement.

The second interpretation seems capable of being reduced to two questions, one likewise of right and one mixed, that is, both of right and of fact. Firstly, whether at a certain point it is lawful for any kingdom to withdraw itself from the obedience of any Pontiff for a time: on which point I know Gerson's resolution, in the question, "How and whether it be lawful in causes per-

nituntur nostrates). Verba ejus sunt §. Sequeretur sexto; *Hoc etiam practicatum est per quoscumque Reges et Principes qui se subtraxerunt ab obedientia illorum, quos isti judicabant esse Summos Pontifices, quæ tamen subtractiones approbatæ sunt per sacrum Constantiense Concil. quædam expresse, quædam implicite vel æquivalenter.* Et sic resolutum dicunt in conventu quodum **Episcoporum Turonensi** in Gallia, quod etiam vidi in hac forma: *Conclusum est per Concilium, Principem posse ab obedientia Papæ se subducere ac subtrahere* (nimirum ob causas gravissimas ibi assignatas) non tamen in totum et indistincte, sed pro tuitione tantum ac defensione jurium suorum temporalium. Quam eorum sententiam, non est meum condemnare, dum Ecclesia tolerat.

Altera est, an fuerint causæ sufficientes in hoc Regno? Factum videmus, sed novimus illud Hieronymi:

taining to the faith to appeal from the Sovereign Pontiff, and to refuse his decision?" (On which Anglicans rely much.) His words are § *Sequeretur sexto*: "This, too, has been often done by certain kings and princes who have withdrawn themselves from the obedience of those whom they believed to be Sovereign Pontiffs, which withdrawals nevertheless were approved by the holy Council of Constance, some expressly, some implicitly, or in an equivalent manner." And they say that this matter was a resolution at a certain meeting of Bishops at Tours, in France, which I too have seen to the following purport: "It has been decided by the Council, that a prince can withdraw himself and depart from the obedience of the Pope" (namely, for certain very weighty causes there assigned), "not however wholly and absolutely, but only for the protection and defence of his temporal rights." Which opinion of theirs it is not for me to condemn while the Church tolerates it.

The second question is, were there sufficient causes in this kingdom? We have seen that it is done, but

Non quæritur an factum, sed an bene factum fuerit.

Hoc tamen dato, licet à nullo Catholico concesso: adhuc quærendum esset, An saltem in modo non excesserint? multa enim de jure licita sunt, cum moderamine inculpatæ tutelæ, ut loquuntur Canones, quæ alias ex intemperantia actionis et defensionis culpas gravissimas subinde non evadunt.

Utraque quæstio sine dubio gravissima est, et maximam à nostratibus meretur discussionem.

Quod si causa sufficiens non fuerit, vel terminos justæ subtractionis excesserint, quanta pericula in tam diuturno schismate! huic utique omnia quantacunque mala sunt, originaliter ebullierunt. Catholici veriori et tutiori parti adhærere volentes, tam insufficientiam causæ, quam moderaminis excessum agnoverunt; ponderant utique gravissimum illud Augustini, *præcidendæ unitatis nulla est justa necessitas*, l. 2, contra ep. Par.

we know that saying of St. Jerome: "The question is not whether the thing be done, but whether it be well done."

But this being granted, though allowed by no Catholic, we should still have to inquire whether they have not gone too far at least in their manner, for many things are lawful, "*cum moderamine inculpatæ tutelæ*" as the Canons say, which otherwise by intemperance in carrying on or defending them do not escape being great faults.

Without doubt each question is most weighty, and deserves especial consideration at the hands of Anglicans.

But if there were not a sufficient cause, or if they exceeded the bounds of a legitimate withdrawal, what peril is there in so long a schism! Hence, indeed, all the evils, how great soever they are, originally burst forth. Catholics, wishing to cleave to the truer and safer part, have recognised both the insufficiency of the cause, and the excess beyond due moderation, besides which they ponder on that most solemn saying of St. Augustine (l. 2, *Cont. ep. Par.*): "No ne-

Utinam denuo, authoritate publica res pro dignitate (Puritanis non intermixtis) ex affectu readunationis perpenderetur, et ad hoc singuli evoluerent Augustinum contra Donatum. Scio illos hoc abhorrere de quibus dicet Cassander (licet haud satis affectus Romanæ Ecclesiæ) de officio pii viri :—*Plerique ex eis, qui sibi ab Evangelio nomen sumpserunt, eam partem quæ vetus Catholicorum et Romanæ Ecclesiæ nomen retinet, prorsus aspernantur, omnemque ejus communionem defugiunt, nec ut membra ejusdem corporis amore et misericordia prosequuntur* (quod nos à Puritanis hic experimur) *sed ut Satanæ et Antichristi corpus abominantur. Scio id equidem et doleo, et qui ejusmodi sunt quomodo à schismatis* (rectius dixisset, hæreseos) *nota eximi possunt, non video.*

Cætera in articulo sunt indubitata.

cessity can justify the breach of unity."

Lastly, would that by public authority the matter as its greatness deserves (Puritans being passed over), were weighed with a desire of reunion. And that to this end every one would study St. Augustine against the Donatists. I know that they hate this, of whom Cassander (though not sufficiently friendly to the Roman Church) says, *de officio pii viri,* "Most of those who have assumed the name Evangelical, wholly despise that portion which retains the ancient name of Catholics and of the Roman Church, and avoid all communion with it, nor do they esteem them with love and gentleness as members of the same body," (which is what we experience here at the hands of the Puritans,) "but eschew them as the body of Satan and of Antichrist. I know that indeed, and grieve over it, nor do I see how persons of that class can be exempted from the charge of schism." (He should more rightly have said heresy.)

The other statements in the Article are irrefragable.

ARTICULUS XXXVIII.—*De illicita bonorum communicatione.*

FACULTATES et bona Christianorum non sunt communia quoad jus et possessionem (ut quidem Anabaptistæ falso jactant); debet tamen quisque de his quæ possidet pro facultatam ratione pauperibus eleemosynas benignè distribuere.

PARAPHRASIS.—Catholicus est et pius.

ARTICULUS XXXIX.—*De jurejurando.*

QUEMAMODUM juramentum vanum et temerarium à Domino nostro Jesu Christo et Apostolo ejus Jacobo, Christianis hominibus interdictum esse fatemur: ita Christianorum Religionem minime prohibere censemus, quin jubente Magistratu in causa Fidei et Charitatis jurare liceat, modo id fiat juxta Prophetæ doctrinam, in justitia, in judicio et veritate.

PARAPHRASIS.—Catholicus est, in Scripturis fundatus, et praxi totius Ecclesiæ stabilitus.

ARTICLE XXXVIII.—*Of Christian men's Goods, which are not common.*

THE Riches and Goods of Christians are not common, as touching the right, title, and possession of the same, as certain Anabaptists do falsely boast. Notwithstanding, every man ought, of such things as he possesseth, liberally to give alms to the poor, according to his ability.

EXPLANATION.—This is Catholic and pious.

ARTICLE XXXIX.—*Of a Christian man's oath.*

AS we confess that vain and rash Swearing is forbidden Christian men by our Lord Jesus Christ, and *James* his Apostle, so we judge, that Christian Religion doth not prohibit, but that a man may swear when the Magistrate requireth, in a cause of faith and charity, so it be done according to the Prophet's teaching, in justice, judgment, and truth.

EXPLANATION.—This is Catholic, founded on Scripture, and established by the practice of the whole Church.

Insudavi, ut vides, pie Lector, reconciliare Articulos Confessionis Anglicæ, determinationibus Ecclesiæ [Rom.] Catholicæ; non Ecclesiam ipsis, ex quâ collapsi sunt; sed ipsos Ecclesiæ, in qua (Dei opitulante gratia) salvandi sunt, reducendos censui. Corticem verborum subinde censurâ graviori dignum censebis, sensum vero **latitantem, quem** elicui, non **adeo veritati dissonum, nisi** aliò **detorquere malint, recti judicabis.** His tamen verborum novitatibus, Christum lacerum inspexi, tunicam inconsutilem, **dissutam,** dissectam, reperi; quis non condoleret? quis non redintegrationem suaderet? omnibus modis, si posset, persuaderet? hic unicus scopus meus. Ad hoc veni ut vides, *non in sublimitate sermonis* (volebam enim mentem, non dictionem componere; rationem, non orationem dirigere) *non asperitate orationis* (absinthia enim melle illiniuntur, ut pellant **morbos**) *sed pietate conciliationis* (charitatis scilicet visceribus, non fictis litibus veritas propugnatur) *palæstram hanc Theologicam in Domino fretus conscendi.*

I have laboured, as you see, pious Reader, to reconcile the Articles of **the Anglican Confession with the decrees of the R. Catholic Church.** I thought that men ought to be brought back to the Church in which (by aid of the grace of God) they must be saved, not the Church whence they have fallen off to them. You will **esteem the bare words sometimes deserving** of a severe censure, but the **hidden sense, which I have** drawn out, you will rightly **esteem not very** dissonant from the truth, except when **men choose to** twist it another **way.** But in these new-fangled expressions I beheld Christ divided; I saw His seamless robe unwoven—torn asunder. Who would not mourn at such a sight? Who would not advise Re-union? Who would not persuade to it by every means which he could? And this was my only object. To this work I came, as you see, *not in loftiness of speech* (for I was more anxious to compose my mind than **my** sentences—to reason than **to show** eloquence), *not in sharpness of speech* (for wormwood is disguised in honey **that disease** may be cured), *but in the anxious*

Omnia Ecclesiæ et ejus sub Christo capiti quâ debeo reverentia submitto, et eo plus, quo dicit Gerson Consid. 2, de Protestatione circa materiam Fidei: *Nullum esse vel fuisse de errore notatum qui sic protestaretur* (aut quod idem est) Ecclesiæ submitteret: ultro obtestor Deum et sanctos ejus, me in hâc qualicumque opellâ nostra, animarum salutem per fidei redintegrationem, intendere. Quod Deus per viscera Domini Nostri Jesu Christi, ad intercessionem omnium Beatorum opportune efficiat; et serenissimum Regem nostrum, *pro omnium Catholicorum votis*, ad utramque felicitatem perducat.

Si fortè inter scribendum subinde falsæ irrepserint citationes, non mirandum: in multis utique ob temporis et loci tenuem commoditatem, non ipsos Authores, quos ad manus non habui, sed exscripta mea, quæ

wish for reconciliation (for the truth is defended by bowels of charity, not by stirring up quarrels); *relying on the Lord, I approached this task of Theology.*

I submit everything, with that respect which I ought, to the Church, and her head under Christ, and that the more for the reason, which Gerson mentions (*Consid. 2, de Protestat. circa mater. fidei*): "No one is or has been charged with error who was willing to make this protestation:" or (which is the same thing) would submit to the Church. And I call God and His Saints to witness, that I intended in this work of mine to effect the salvation of souls by the restoration of faith. Which may God, through the mercy of our Lord Jesus Christ, grant in His good time to the intercession of all the Blessed, and bring our most gracious King (*according to the wishes of all Catholics*) to both those blessings.

It must not be a matter of surprise if some false quotations should have crept into this work, since in many cases, from the imperfect convenience either of time or place, I did not consult the authors them-

ob corruptionem characterem aliquando vix legere licuit, consului. Huic etiam accedit, me amanuensis subsidio, nempe ut littera prælo accommodatior fieret, semper usum, quem ob ignorantiam, errores etiam graviores exiliisse, non raro adverti. De prælo vero quid non timendum ubi ob loci distantiam, nec Authori, ut correctioni impressionis libere intendat, fas est? Sancte tamen dico, me nunquam ut à partibus nostris stet ullum authorem pervertisse, vel detruncasse, *pro veritate enim non nisi veritate certandum.*

selves, whom I had not at hand, but my own extracts, which from the great illegibility of the writing I sometimes could hardly read. Besides this, in order that the manuscript might be more fit for the press, I made use of a writer, from whose ignorance I have perceived that sometimes even grave mistakes have crept in. But what must not be feared for the printing, when on account of distance the Author has been unable to attend to the correction as much as was required? I will say, however, with a good conscience, that I have nowhere perverted or mutilated any author that he might be on my side, *for in striving for the truth we ought not to strive except with truth.*

The following Works, representing the Re-union School, and bearing on the Re-union Movement in England and elsewhere, can be ordered of the Publisher,

MR. J. T. HAYES,

LYALL PLACE, EATON SQUARE, LONDON, S.W.

I.

Publishing, in Nos., once in Two Months, price 2s.; by Post 2s. 2d.

THE UNION REVIEW.

A MAGAZINE OF CATHOLIC LITERATURE AND ART.

"Marked by considerable ability. The article on 'Re-union' is very ably written."—*Guardian.*

"The organ of the Re-unionist school in the Anglican Church, and one which is distinguished for brilliancy, depth, and theological learning."—*Levant Herald.*

"In length and ability the articles in this Magazine will rival those in the more ambitious and expensive quarterlies."—*Churchman.*

"This most interesting periodical."—*Church Review.*

"The force and brilliancy of its political articles (always lively reading) are undoubtedly marked features in this clever serial.—*British Review.*

"The 'Literary Notices' struck us as **remarkably well done**. . . . . It opens with an article of very considerable ability."—*John Bull.*

"The 'Union Review' possesses in a high degree all these interesting features. A distinguished literary and theological authority."—*Jersey Times.*

"A most interesting number.   It fills up a vacant space in religious literature well and successfully."—*Oxford Journal.*

"The 'Coming Contest at Oxford' is one of those brilliant political articles for which this Magazine is rapidly gaining a character."—*Church Times.*

*** A few Copies of Vols. I. and II. are still to be had, 13s. 6d. each. Those who are desirous of securing complete sets should apply at once to the Publisher. Vol. III., handsomely bound in cloth, will be ready in November, 1865.

II.

Price 1s.; by Post 1s. 1d.

THE UNION REVIEW ALMANACK.

AN ECCLESIASTICAL KALENDAR FOR THE YEAR OF GRACE 1866.

This Almanack, in addition to the usual contents of such a publication, contains full directions for the Celebration of Divine Service, according to the Use of the Church of England, rendering it a perfect *vade mecum* for the Clergy, while it will be found equally valuable to Sacristans, Cantors, Parish Clerks, Servers, and others assisting in the Service of the Sanctuary.

CRITIQUES ON THE FORMER ISSUE.

"This is a very valuable addition to our Ecclesiastical almanacks."—*Church Review*

"We recommend this Kalendar for its Notitia Liturgica."—*Church Times.*

"The most complete Church of England Calendar issued, and very reasonable in cost.—*Oxford Herald.*

"A most useful and admirable Kalendar."—*John Bull.*

"The Ritual Notices are very elaborate."—*The Churchman.*

III.

In Foolscap, 8vo., price 5s.; by Post 5s. 4d.

SERMONS ON THE RE-UNION OF CHRISTENDOM.

FIRST SERIES.

BY MEMBERS OF THE ROMAN CATHOLIC, ORIENTAL, AND ANGLICAN COMMUNIONS.

[LONDON: MASTERS AND CO.]

"The Sermons are very far above the average of ordinary discourses, and contain thoughts, and food for thought, sufficient to stock preachers on the subject for months. We commend the book very cordially to our readers' attention."—*The Churchman.*

"The publication of this volume forms an epoch in the Church Revival of this generation."—*Ecclesiastic.*

"There are passages, and those not a few, in these Sermons, of the greatest truth and beauty."—*Bishop Ullathorne's Letter on the A.P.U.C.*

"Eloquent passages, showing forth the evils of schism."—*Record.*

"There is a devout, and peaceful, and loving temper diffused over the whole."—*Clerical Journal.*

"A more able volume has not appeared of late."—*Church Times.*

"Contains little which might not have been written by any earnest Churchman."—*Guardian.*

"Much of eloquence, much of power and thought, much of loving earnestness as it contains, yet it is chiefly attractive in being, from the circumstances under which it was produced and put together, the most remarkable fruit of English origin since the Reformation."—*Church Review.*

"In every respect, it may be regarded as a singular success."—*Union Review.*

"The most remarkable volume of Sermons we have seen for years."—*Herald.*

"The title of this remarkable book sufficiently explains its character and scope. Much that is said throughout the volume by each writer will commend itself to every Christian man. Without in any way committing ourselves to the line of argument of some of the Sermons, we recommend the book with cordiality."—*John Bull.*

IV.

Price 5s.; by Post 5s. 4d.

THE SECOND SERIES
OF
SERMONS ON THE RE-UNION OF CHRISTENDOM.

BY MEMBERS OF THE ENGLISH, ROMAN, AND GREEK CHURCHES.

"We recall the first series of these Sermons with feelings of admiration and enjoyment. This second series is a fit continuation of the first. Their eloquence, charity, and argumentative ability, are as striking as their object is high and admirable. The Sermons before us, which will, we doubt not, be largely read in the East as well as at home, will conduce to the advance of charity, soundness of doctrine, and Unity They go far to solve the problem, on the solution of which the future of all Christian communities depends, viz., how to reconcile the two principles of Dogma and Unity, how to make unswerving adherence to truth compatible with brotherhood and love. It is only grace that can do this. But the discussion of disputed doctrines in a loving spirit and kind tone will do much to help the work of grace. This method of setting forth their views the writers of these Sermons have fully adopted. They are conceived in the truest spirit of charity, and yet they assert strongly all necessary truths. The names which are appended to some of the Sermons, or are suggested by the initials of others, furnish an à priori ground for expecting that this would be the case. It is a hard task to select where there is so much that is forcible and so much that is eloquent."—*The Churchman.*

"This is a volume of great beauty and excellence, and one which is not only worth reading but worth keeping. Many of the sermons in it are of rare order, which makes you put them by to be read again and again, not so much in your hours of energy and activity, as in those hours when you feel the need of that peculiar spiritual and mental stimulus which arises from the contemplation of high thoughts well uttered.—*Literary Churchman.*

"These sermons seem to us of much more practical value than those which were first published. They each point to some definite effort, which even individuals may make towards the great end in view. The majority of them are above the average in ability."—*Ecclesiastic.*

"Although one or two of the sermons in the earlier series were fully equal, in point of literary ability, to the best of those in the volume before us, yet if we were to take stock of the contents of both series, as regards general merit, we should award the palm to the contributions furnished to the late issue. . . . . . There is a fine sermon of Mr. Carter's, and another contributed by Mr. Bennett."—*Church Times.*

"Let us now regard these Sermons, and we shall find much to instruct and benefit us."—*Clerical Journal.*

V.

Price 3d.; by Post 4d.

PRAYERS FOR THE RE-UNION OF CHRISTENDOM.

COMPILED BY THE SECRETARY OF THE A.P.U.C.
APPROVED BY ENGLISH, GREEK, ROMAN, SCOTTISH, AND COLONIAL BISHOPS.

VI.

Price 1s.; by Post 1s. 1d.

THE

FUTURE UNITY OF THE CHRISTIAN FAMILY.

A SERMON PREACHED AT ALL SAINTS, MARGARET STREET, CAVENDISH SQUARE, ON SEPTEMBER 8, 1865.

By REV. T. T. CARTER, M.A., RECTOR OF CLEWER.

WITH

An Appendix, containing a Report of the A.P.U.C., and its Progress, by the Secretary.

VII.

Price 1s.; by Post 1s. 1d.

THE

EXPERIENCES OF A 'VERT (CONVERT).

REPRINTED FROM "THE UNION REVIEW."

"Interesting from the rare power of being honest which the writer shows, and from the fact which he points out and bears witness to."—*Guardian.*

"Most valuable and interesting; equal in these points to Dr. Newman's *Apologia.*"—*Daily Mail.*

VIII.

Preparing for Publication, 8vo.

ESSAYS ON THE RE-UNION OF CHRISTENDOM.

BY MEMBERS OF THE ROMAN CATHOLIC, ORIENTAL, AND ANGLICAN COMMUNIONS.

EDITED BY THE REV. F. G. LEE.

NEW WORKS also recently Published by
J. T. HAYES.

I.
THE BIBLE AND ITS INTERPRETERS.

I. THE POPULAR THEORY. III. THE LITERARY THEORY.
II. THE ROMAN THEORY. IV. THE TRUTH.

By REV. W. J. IRONS, D.D., PREBENDARY OF ST. PAUL'S.

"This is, on the whole, a very remarkable book. We heartily commend this treatise to the attention especially of our clerical brethren, and of all who take an interest in the deep subjects it so ably grapples with."—*Church Review.*

II.
Price 3s.; by Post 3s. 4d.

THE REFORMED MONASTERY; OR THE LOVE OF JESUS:

A Sure and Short, Pleasant and Easy Way to Heaven; in Meditations, Directions, and Resolutions to Love and Obey JESUS unto Death.

Edited with a PREFACE by the REV. F. G. LEE, D.C.L., F.S.A., Domestic Chaplain to the Earl of Morton.

(Being a Reprint of the said Work by Dr. BOILEAU, Chaplain to Dr. FELL, Bishop of Oxford, 1675.)

III.
ce 1s.; by Post 1s. 1d.

HOUSEHOLD PRAYERS:

With a PREFACE by the RIGHT REV. THE LORD BISHOP OF OXFORD.

The Profits of this Work to be devoted to the Workwomen in Sickness connected with the London Dressmaking Company.

IV.

Price 1s. 6d.; by Post 1s. 7d.

ON THE

DUTIES OF FATHERS AND MOTHERS.

By ARVISENET.

Edited by REV. G. C. WHITE, S. Barnabas', Pimlico.

V.

Sixth Edition, price 8d.; by Post 9d.

THE

RHYTHM OF BERNARD OF MORLAIX,

CONCERNING THE HEAVENLY COUNTRY.

Edited and Translated by the REV. J. M. NEALE, D.D.

VI.

Also, a Companion Volume to the above, price 1s. 6d.; by Post 1s. 7d.

HYMNS

(Chiefly Mediæval)

ON THE JOYS AND GLORIES OF PARADISE.

By the REV. J. M. NEALE, D.D.

VII.

Price 2s. 6d.; by Post 2s. 7d.

THE

HYMNS OF THE EASTERN CHURCH.

Translated by the REV. J. M. NEALE, D.D.

J. T. HAYES, LYALL PLACE, EATON SQUARE.

www.ingramcontent.com/pod-product-compliance
Lightning Source LLC
Chambersburg PA
CBHW030303170426
43202CB00009B/858